ACCESSING YOUR
ANOINTING

PASTOR GREG LOCKE

Global Vision Press™

CHARISMA
HOUSE

ACCESSING YOUR ANOINTING by Greg Locke
Published by Charisma House, an imprint of Charisma Media
600 Rinehart Road, Lake Mary, Florida 32746

Unless otherwise noted, all Scripture is taken from the King James Version of the Holy Bible.

Scripture quotations marked ESV are from the Holy Bible, English Standard Version. Copyright © 2001 by Crossway Bibles, a division of Good News Publishers. Used by permission.

Cover photo and design by Wayne Caparas contact@LockeMedia.org

While the author has made every effort to provide accurate internet addresses at the time of publication, neither the publisher nor the author assumes any responsibility for errors or for changes that occur after publication. Further, the publisher does not have any control over and does not assume any responsibility for author or third-party websites or their content.

For more Spirit-led resources, visit charismamedia.com and the author's website at LockeMedia.org.

Cataloging-in-Publication Data is on file with the Library of Congress.

International Standard Book Number: 978-1-63641-345-7
E-book ISBN: 978-1-63641-346-4

23 24 25 26 27 — 987654321
Printed in the United States of America

Most Charisma Media products are available at special quantity discounts for bulk purchases for sales promotions, premiums, fundraising, and educational needs. For details, call us at (407) 333-0600 or visit our website at www.charismamedia.com.

Charisma House gratefully acknowledges the partnership of Global Vision Press in the publication of this book.

DEDICATION

This book is affectionately dedicated to my "Granny and Paw Paw." Although both are in heaven now, they have a legacy in my ministry to this day.

Granny prayed fervently for my salvation and was the first person to ever speak a word over me that I would be a preacher. She taught me kindness and compassion. The Lord kept her alive just long enough to see her prayers answered.

Paw Paw was a fearless warrior that had no regard for the opinions of others, and he instilled in me a boldness and a fire that God has used mightily. I often say, "I simply open my mouth, and my grandfather walks out." His was the very first funeral I ever preached. These two beautiful people still have a major influence on my life, and my sermons are filled with quotations and wisdom that both imparted to me. I miss them dearly, but I'm eternally grateful for their voice in my life and ministry.

CONTENTS

CONTENTS

Foreword

I HAD THE OPPORTUNITY to travel the nation with Pastor Greg Locke during the 2020 lockdowns. Together, we have preached the gospel of the kingdom of God from the East Coast to the West. I've spent months with him on the road. During this time, I've had a front-row seat to see that he is more than just a friend; he is also a patriot and, most importantly, a man of God.

As we traveled together, he diligently searched the Scriptures on the topic of the Holy Spirit. Having come from a cessationist background, he wanted to see for himself if the gifts of the Spirit, and the activity of the Holy Spirit, were still alive and well in the church today like they were in the Book of Acts.

None of our theologies are fully perfect. Every day we should sit as a student, seeking the counsel of Almighty God. I know that my theology is still being perfected and refined. It's very easy to get trapped in the theology you have already accepted, but as I have watched Greg study with a genuine hunger for the truth and desire to have all that God has for him and his congregation, I have been humbled by his willingness to let God teach and correct him.

I've seen Greg embrace a belief system that is scriptural, practical, and powerful. A belief system that is available for every New Testament believer. I believe the words in this book will be encouraging and inspiring and will unleash your anointing in a new and fresh way that will help a lost and dying world.

—PASTOR BRIAN GIBSON

INTRODUCTION

*The Spirit of the Lord is upon me, because he hath anointed
me to preach the gospel to the poor; he hath sent me to heal
the brokenhearted, to preach deliverance to the captives, and
recovering of sight to the blind, to set at liberty them that
are bruised, to preach the acceptable year of the Lord.*
—JESUS (LUKE 4:18–19)

I'M A WORD man—a Bible guy. You have to convince me using
the Bible. Your experiences don't convince me. Fiery charismatic
preachers don't convince me. Televised shows, media reports, tear-
jerking stories, colorful allegories, and academic commentaries
don't ultimately convince me. The Bible alone convinces and con-
victs me of truth; only the Bible can change my mind about my biblical beliefs. This little book was born of one of those changes.

1

I also love Jesus with every fiber, breath, and thought. I'm in love with Him through and through, and I want more of Him in me, not less. This desire is the bottom line of this book.

When the ongoing global chaos was in its early stages, the subject of this book wouldn't let me rest. The Holy Spirit was doing a new work in me, and I knew I had to shout about it from the rooftops.

He then showed me He was raising an army that needed to suit up and boot up for battle against the enemy's schemes. This need birthed what has now become the first book in this Spiritual Warfare Series, *Weapons of Our Warfare,* where we dive deep into God's strategies for spiritual battle and His power in the armor of God. It's no coincidence that I start this third book where the second left off, with Jesus standing before a hostile crowd in His home church, preparing to launch His ministry (Luke 4:18–19).

In that historic moment, Jesus proclaimed the supernatural works that mark His church, then and now. If you open your Bible and read it again in context, you'll see He read the Isaiah 61:1 commission straight out of the scrolls. This beautiful proclamation was initially for Him, but now it's for us.

Most folks in the church sit in confusion about the power of the Holy Spirit, as most pastors are unwilling to risk discussing power they don't believe exists today. Even among those who do, few compel their congregations to access it. What about you? Is the supernatural power of the gifts of the Spirit still available to you today, or not? This book will help you answer that question and many more.

A Journey Worth Taking

> Now he which stablisheth us with you in Christ, and hath
> anointed us, is God; who hath also sealed us, and given the
> earnest of the Spirit in our hearts.
>
> —2 Corinthians 1:21–22

My personal beliefs have always left room for an outpouring of the
Holy Spirit's anointing in the last days (Joel 2:28; Acts 2:17), and I
have long believed the last of the last days are already upon us. For
this, I've been eager to learn how to fully access this outpouring
and how to properly put it into action. I also wanted to know—
once and for all—whether I was right to have ever taught that the
gifts of the Spirit had become unnecessary and void at some point
in the past.

To answer that uncomfortable question, I looked deep into the
apostle Paul's writings about the gifts, revisited the red letters of
Jesus in full, and studied all of Scripture to root out every related
gem I could find. When I came through the other side of my search,
the Bible had corrected me on several undeniable truths about the
gifts. I've never been so glad to be so wrong. This book will make a
few of you nervous, and that's okay.

Confession of a Former Cessationist

> Jesus answered and said unto them, Ye do err, not knowing
> the scriptures, nor the power of God.
>
> —Matthew 22:29

Jesus delivered this piercing rebuke to hypocritical religious scholars
trying to snare Him with misappropriated scriptures they didn't
even understand. Sadly, religious hypocrites are still playing that
wordplay game today. Despite having no real biblical basis, many
denominations and sects decided long ago that they simply *ceased*
at some point after the days of the first-century apostles.

Theologically, we call this disempowering doctrine *cessationism*.

Like most Baptists, I was raised to be a stringent cessationist. As a seminary-trained evangelist and pastor, I remained a *dyed-in-the-wool*, fully committed proponent of cessationism for most of my ministry life. But when I removed those old lenses and finally looked behind the denominational curtain with open eyes, the error was easy to see.

It's important that you know this revelatory shift in my theology wasn't prompted by a dream, spoken word, or prophetic vision—though I received much confirmation through each of these. Instead, it came through black words on white paper in the Bible (along with plenty of red letters) and nothing more.

Where the gifts of the Spirit are concerned, either the Bible is right or my seminary is right. They simply do not agree on this crucial issue. Unless you want to argue that my denomination or your denomination has authority over the Bible, you have no choice but to agree. You can believe what the Bible says, and you can also believe what your grandfather says, but if they disagree on a particular issue, you'd better know your grandpa is wrong. The same is true for your grandpa's denomination and my own.

To put it plainly, the Bible says that the gifts of the Spirit are available to the very end, so I must repent of my cessationist past. I know this will upset some of my Baptist friends, but if you (and they) give this book a chance, I believe you'll be convinced of this same truth. I also believe you'll agree that we desperately need to access the spiritual gifts more now than ever.

A Consuming Fire

I hope you'll dial in with me for what I write next. This book is about the Holy Spirit in us—*God in us*. Yes, this book is about the anointing and the spiritual gifts, but don't miss the fundamental truth about those subjects. Both speak to the reality of the Holy Spirit of God literally living inside us.

Let's connect with what that means. This isn't a Marvel comic book story or some sort of new-age hocus-pocus. We're talking about our Living God's active, supernatural, power-packed life in us.

The Bible tells us that God exists as a consuming fire over and within a believer; He is a holy fire that empowers and refines us. When I mention the anointing, power, or gifts of the Spirit, always remember that I'm talking about the Holy Spirit within us, Christ within us—God within us—and nothing less. Embracing the power and fire of His presence is an act of worship, and we all need to worship Him with reverence in this regard.

> Wherefore we receiving a kingdom which cannot be moved, let us have grace, whereby we may serve God acceptably with reverence and godly fear: For our God is a consuming fire.
> —HEBREWS 12:28–29

The Power and the Process

If you're a student of the Scripture, you already know that holy men of God "spake" and wrote the words we find in the Bible as the Holy Spirit moved them. The Word of God is not man's opinion but God's exposition of Himself—His character, His nature, and His commands—for the purpose of our regenerative salvation through relationship with Him. Sadly, this regenerative process has become very unpopular in the lukewarm church today. It seems everyone wants the power, but no one wants the process.

For this, most churches and Christians cherry-pick the Bible, and cessationists have done this for centuries. They've ignored or discounted large portions of the Bible that they believe have expired. But the Bible is not a buffet with food that gets thrown out when it's no longer wanted. Our beliefs and actions are our expression (and evidence) of whether we truly believe the *whole* Bible, and no man or denomination can claim that any of God's scriptural promises are suddenly obsolete.

The Bible unites us, so we need to address this openly as the body of Christ. If we continue side-stepping or dumbing down the subject of this book, it won't just keep the church divided; it will remain a point of contention and division between the church and God. His promises are either unchanging or they are not.

> The grass withereth, the flower fadeth: but the word of our
> God shall stand for ever.
>
> —ISAIAH 40:8

The Error of the Lawless

In his sobering second letter to the church, the apostle Peter compelled us to diligently study and adhere to Paul's writings, no matter how mysterious or difficult. In this epistle, Peter warns us that if we fail to properly interpret Paul's writings or are led away by the erroneous teachings of men, we risk misinterpreting the whole Bible to our demise. After discussing the realities of the judgment to come, Peter delivered this stern warning:

> Wherefore, beloved, seeing that ye look for such things, be diligent that ye may be found of him in peace, without spot, and blameless. And account that the longsuffering of our Lord is salvation; even as our beloved brother Paul also according to the wisdom given unto him hath written unto you; As also in all his epistles, speaking in them of these things; in which are some things hard to be understood, which they that are unlearned and unstable wrest, as they do also the other scriptures, unto their own destruction. Ye therefore, beloved, seeing ye know these things before, beware lest ye also, being

led away with the error of the wicked, fall from your own
stedfastness.

—2 PETER 3:14–17

Misusing Scripture is a lawless, wicked practice, no matter how
sincere we may be in our motives. We need to "be diligent" and
"take care" to ensure we're not swept up in such error. The devil
uses deception and wordplay to twist the Word of God at every
opportunity. (See Genesis 3:4; Matthew 4:6.) And he aggressively
seduces the people of God with scriptural confusion to advance his
schemes.

In Peter's foreboding passage, God warns us of this destructive
snare. Lawless, wicked men were twisting Paul's words in ways that
discredited the patience and the power of the Lord.

Many are still doing this today. Having the Bible firmly in hand,
I can blame no man for my lack of understanding, and neither can
you. Every bucket sits on its own bottom, so it's time we each take
personal responsibility to root out biblical error in every area of
our lives.

I don't believe the elders and professors at my seminary are now,
or ever were, lawless by intent. The same can be said of the great
thinkers of old who trained up my theology through their sermons
and books. But at some point in church history, wicked, lawless,
"unlearned and unstable" men sowed confusion into many of Paul's
most mysterious writings, just as God forewarned.

In the centuries that followed, all the denominational hierarchies
that ascribed to their errors have found themselves in grave danger
of missing the manifest power of God when most needed. We're
presently reaping confusion sown by the lawless, and we'll continue
to do so until we get it right.

How Did We Get It So Wrong?

If you're wondering how my seminary and many denominations got it so wrong, there are myriad irrational reasons based in ignorance and control. For our study, however, it's far more important to uncover how they misused the Bible to justify their error than to dissect their motives.

The cessationist doctrine teeters on a single, terribly misinterpreted prophecy that Paul penned in his first epistle (letter) to the church in Corinth. Let's give it a serious look so we can end the debate right here in this extended Introduction.

> Charity never faileth: but whether there be prophecies, they shall fail; whether there be tongues, they shall cease; whether there be knowledge, it shall vanish away. For we know in part, and we prophesy in part. But when that which is perfect is come, then that which is in part shall be done away.
> —1 CORINTHIANS 13:8–10

If you're new to the Bible or have never studied this particular passage, let me explain that Paul is pointing to a momentous future event that will occur somewhere on the Bible's prophetic timeline. If you were never indoctrinated into cessationist theology, I'd expect that it's obvious that Paul was writing a last of the last days prophecy. Yet, cessationists believe the phrase, "when that which is perfect is come," somehow refers to the gathering and printing of the first complete English Bible. If you're not a cessationist, I'd bet that sounds silly to you. It finally sounds silly to me too.

Cessationism begs the question: What could possibly make the first complete *English* Bible so pivotal to God? After all, God speaks Spanish and Swahili. As an English-speaking Baptist who teaches from the King James Bible, that theory sounded cool when I was a young seminary student, but it sounds ridiculous today. That slanted theory simply does not line up with the whole of Scripture or the character and power of God.

Don't Blame the Bible

To be specific, most theologians who teach cessationism believe that Paul was prophesying the year 1611 when the King James Version (KJV) of the Bible was first printed. According to them, that's when all the gifts ceased, and they hung it all on that single passage above to come to that conclusion. To borrow from Jesus' rebuke in Matthew 22:29, they neither understand this Scripture nor have proper respect for the power of God in us.

As you may have noticed, I dearly love the KJV. In *Weapons of Our Warfare*, I paid homage to the historic events that led up to its publication in 1611. I'll be the last man to discount its historic or spiritual significance. Nonetheless, it betrays the whole Bible to believe that the English language or the first assembly of the KJV could somehow disarm born-again believers of supernatural power given to us by God.

To those who still propagate that nonsense, I want to point out that Dr. Bottlestopper might have told you that, and Sister Wigglejaw might have told you that, but the apostle Paul never told you that. The Bible never told you that. God never told you that!

> All scripture is given by inspiration of God, and is profitable for doctrine, for reproof, for correction, for instruction in righteousness: That the man of God may be perfect, thoroughly furnished unto all good works.
> —2 Timothy 3:16–17

As Paul wrote in his second letter to Timothy, all Scripture is profitable for every good work, no matter the language, translation, quantity, or mode of transfer. This promise never expires. Jesus never made a promise to His bride (the church) that can be voided by the actions or decisions of mere men. Why would He reduce the power of His indwelling? He wouldn't.

When we operate in obedience, God is always expanding and never shrinking. John the Baptist stated this same fact when he said, "He must increase, but I must decrease" (John 3:30). God promises to equip us for every good work, and He will always keep His Word (Num. 23:19). All of God's promises are yes and amen (2 Cor. 1:20).

Keeping It in Context

> For now we see through a glass, darkly; but then face to face:
> now I know in part; but then shall I know even as also I am
> known.
>
> —1 CORINTHIANS 13:12

Have you ever noticed that you could read a passage of Scripture a hundred times, then suddenly you read it, and revelation jumps off the page? For me, this verse provided a beautiful example of that phenomenon. The meaning was always there, but I had to remove my foggy denominational lenses to see it clearly.

Confusion concerning a single passage of Scripture can often be cleared up with an honest, contextual reading of the full passage, chapter, epistle, or book that contains it. Considering the centuries of cessationist confusion, it may surprise you that Paul gave us that clarity within the very chapter that has been so badly misinterpreted.

Immediately after mentioning "that which is perfect," Paul uses the metaphor of a child becoming a man to highlight the dramatic transformation we will experience when the perfect finally comes (v. 11). Through this, God is saying that the perfect event—in contrast with our current state—would transform us into a much wiser, far more powerful form.

Then Paul delivered verse 12 (above) with undeniable intent. Not only has the perfect day not yet come, but when it does come, born-again believers will be transformed to fully know His power and to fully see God face to face, no longer "in part." When Paul wrote that these partial gifts would one day "vanish away," he wasn't saying there would be a cessation of power among the bride of Christ but a graduation of power from partial glory to the fullness of glory. In his second letter to the church at Corinth, Paul reiterates this truth about the Holy Spirit's transforming power while proving that it applies to every born-again believer with no exceptions:

> But we all, with open face beholding as in a glass the glory of the Lord, are changed into the same image from glory to glory, even as by the Spirit of the Lord.
>
> —2 CORINTHIANS 3:18

What Is "That Which Is Perfect"?

Knowing all this, we can fully trust that Paul's perfect event represents the apocalyptic day of Jesus' return (judgment day), "the great and notable" day of the Lord that Peter prophesied (Acts 2:20). But let's be clear: "that which is perfect" is not referring to Jesus Himself, rather the perfecting effect that His return will initiate on all the world and every soul in it. It may sound like I'm splitting hairs, but every word in the Bible matters to me, and Jesus is simply not a "that."

If you search the Scripture, you'll find dozens of direct prophetic references to this day, and though it will be a terrible day for unbelievers, it will be perfect for the saved. On the day of the Lord, there will no longer be a need for the partial gifts of the Spirit, for we will be transformed into something far greater.

> In a moment, in the twinkling of an eye, at the last trump: for the trumpet shall sound, and the dead shall be raised incorruptible, and we shall be changed.
>
> —1 CORINTHIANS 15:52

This is the day we will see "the Son of man coming in the clouds of heaven with power and great glory" to claim His bride. It's the day so perfect that Jesus will send His angels to gather every born-again believer into His presence (Matt. 24:30–31). It's the day so perfect that the faithful who died before us will rise from the grave to join Him (John 5:28–29). It's the day so perfect that all evil, wickedness, and lawlessness will be exposed and punished (Isa. 13:9–11). It's the day so perfect that all the saints will be glorified to live with Christ for all eternity (Phil. 3:21; 1 Cor. 15:52), and we will see Jesus "face to face." Could there be a more perfect day? Surely not.

> Beloved, now are we the sons of God, and it doth not yet appear what we shall be: but we know that, when he shall appear, we shall be like him; for we shall see him as he is.
>
> —1 JOHN 3:2

The Great and Awesome Day

If there is urgency baked into my books, it's found in the fact that we are saved and anointed for a rescue mission, not mere self-improvement. Knowing that the judgment begins with hellish, awe-striking implications for most (Isa. 13:9), we can't just sit on our gifting and wait for His return. Jesus' Olivet Discourse speaks directly to the fact that we must preach the gospel and bless the lost with increasing boldness as the day of the Lord approaches (Matt. 24 and 25).

This truth is at the core of Jesus' Great Commission (Matt. 28:19–20), so we must make every effort to help as many souls as possible escape eternity in hell (Jas. 5:20). This is not optional—it is a command—and as you'll see in this book, the gifts of the Spirit are crucial to that mission.

> For the Son of man is come to seek and to save that which was lost.
>
> —JESUS (LUKE 19:10)

Jesus and the Outpouring

In all His mentions of the Holy Spirit's power in us, not once did Jesus say it would face any sort of reduction or cessation before His return. In every instance, He spoke in terms that proved the anointing would never diminish in power. He also reassures us that every born-again believer in every generation would receive this power—even those of us who live in the twenty-first century. Through His final discourse on the night before His crucifixion, He said:

> If ye love me, keep my commandments. And I will pray the Father, and he shall give you another Comforter, that he may abide with you for ever; Even the Spirit of truth; whom the world cannot receive, because it seeth him not, neither knoweth him: but ye know him; for he dwelleth with you, and shall be in you. I will not leave you comfortless: I will come to you.
>
> —JOHN 14:15–18

With this, Jesus dropped what should be the final Word on the subject. "Comforter" and "Spirit of truth" are names Jesus uses for the Holy Spirit. Jesus said the Holy Spirit would forever abide in those who receive Him (born again of the Spirit)—no exceptions, exclusions, limitations, or cessations.

Shortly after His resurrection, He reiterated, "You will receive power when the Holy Spirit has come upon you," and there was no mention of an expiration date (Acts 1:8). One would have to dismiss these red-letter passages (and many others) to believe the Holy Spirit would break His promises and cease to operate through us when we need Him most. Such a concept betrays everything we know about God.

He will never abandon us, and He will never leave us as orphans (John 14:18). Imagine the power that awaits the world once the church fully embraces His consuming fire and openly operates in the anointing—glory to God!

> Let your light so shine before men, that they may see your
> good works, and glorify your Father which is in heaven.
> —JESUS (MATTHEW 5:16)

Upward and Onward

As we turn to our expository study of the spiritual gifts, please put to rest any doubts you may have about your access to the anointing. The power of God will *never* diminish in a spiritually healthy host, and no doctrine of men or demons can change that (Eph. 4:14). For this, if you see a lack of tangible Holy Spirit power in your church, there is likely a shortage of legitimate born-again believers among the leadership. If you can't fire up your pastor, you need to find a new one.

There have always been fake Christians in the ministry, and many are spreading fear, confusion, and false doctrines to justify their unbiblical submission to lawlessness and wicked tyranny. It's evidence of the devil's final push to kill the lost and destroy the church before Jesus returns. For this, the Lord is thinning out the ranks and raising an army (Judg. 7:4–7), and I pray you're ready to stand with us.

A Journey of Growth

I promise to remain transparent about my understanding and personal growth as I continue this journey of discovery into the supernatural anointing of God. I'll admit that I'm still figuring out my personal mix of gifts. I'm still discovering what's in my bag of supernaturally charged abilities and what it looks like to put it all into action in my church and the body of Christ. Yes, I'm called to preach and give generously, but I now know I've left a lot of untapped power on the table during my life. This is probably true for you as well.

Even if you weren't raised to follow the cessationist doctrine, you have likely ignored your spiritual giftedness. But don't beat yourself up, and don't let the enemy trip you into thinking you can change the past. Instead, we all need to set our eyes and hearts on Him as we prepare for the great and awesome day of the Lord. It's time to get right with Him and His Word and get on with our Father's business!

The fact that you are reading this book is evidence that the Holy Spirit is calling you upward to stand against evil and walk in your anointing with fire in your belly. I pray this book provokes you to access your spiritual gifts for good works in battle. The perfect day of the Lord will come like a thief in the night (Matt. 24:42–44). Are you and your loved ones ready?

> And let us consider one another to provoke unto love and to good works: Not forsaking the assembling of ourselves together, as the manner of some is; but exhorting one another: and so much the more, as ye see the day approaching.
> —HEBREWS 10:24–25

1

What Are Spiritual Gifts?

Every good gift and every perfect gift is from above, and
cometh down from the Father of lights, with whom
is no variableness, neither shadow of turning.
—JAMES 1:17

I NEED TO STATE this plainly up front and restate it as often as possible: The supernatural power in the spiritual gifts comes only through the anointing of the Holy Spirit. In short, the gifts of the Spirit (a.k.a. spiritual gifts) are supernatural abilities that God uses through us to bless individuals and the church. God alone gives the gifts—as He pleases to whom He pleases. No human can transfer the gifts or give them to others. Though some have the gifting to recognize and encourage spiritual gifts and thereby compel their proper use (to *impart*, Rom. 1:11), no man or woman can anoint anyone with the Holy Spirit (God). Only God can do that.

God bestows certain gifts upon every human at birth, but these gifts aren't anointed with Holy Spirit power until the Holy Spirit lives within us through the born-again life. These natural-born gifts can be viewed as the good gifts God speaks of in the Book of James (above). This anointing makes the gift "perfect," as James notes.

Among the most celebrated spiritual gifts are knowledge, faith, healing, prophecy, and miracles, but there are many more. I'll restate it here and often: As is true of the armor of God, the Holy Spirit is the only power source of the gifts of the Spirit. All else is counterfeit and demonic. More on that later.

What Is the Anointing?

God has been anointing men and women with Holy Spirit power from the beginning, but the widespread access to gifts of the Spirit began fifty days after the resurrection on the day of Pentecost. On that day, Holy Spirit fire fell in a new way, and thousands were born again in a night.

You may notice that I use the word *anointing* and the phrase *gifts of the Spirit* somewhat interchangeably. I do that for good reason. In the original manuscripts, the Greek word *charisma* is the root word for both, making them practically synonymous.

The root word for *charisma* is the word *charis*, which means the grace of God. In English, *grace* is the unmerited favor of God. From this, we see that the anointing of the spiritual gifts is freely given once we are born again. It may take effort and boldness to *access* them, but as this word study reveals, no amount of work can *earn* them.

Like many words, the word *anointing* has more than one meaning in the Bible. The common use of the word deals with the rubbing or pouring of oil or other substances as a blessing. Any believer can do that sort of anointing, and it's a beautiful act when performed in the right spirit. Both forms deal with matters of God, but only God anoints with the Holy Spirit and power (Acts 1:8).

In the Book of Acts, the apostle Peter had a profound discussion with the Roman centurion Cornelius, where he explained God's anointing in the most powerful way possible—as expressed through the life of Jesus:

> That word, I say, ye know, which was published throughout all Judaea, and began from Galilee, after the baptism which John preached; How God anointed Jesus of Nazareth with the Holy Ghost and with power: who went about doing good, and healing all that were oppressed of the devil; for God was with him.
>
> —ACTS 10:37–38

While Jesus was fully God from the very beginning, He walked out every aspect of the human experience to show us the way, the truth, and the life that every born-again believer must follow and obey (John 14:6). So, don't be surprised by the fact that Jesus received this same anointing from God before He began working miracles and doing other good works.

Must We Be Born Again?

> Jesus answered, Verily, verily, I say unto thee, Except a man be born of water and of the Spirit, he cannot enter into the kingdom of God.
>
> —JESUS (JOHN 3:5)

If you follow my preaching online, you might have noticed that I'm on a bit of a mission to cast light on true salvation and what it means to be born again. We have far too many fake Christians in the ministry, and that wickedness is of the devil. In the revelatory third chapter of the Gospel of John, Jesus teaches a non-negotiable process that the church has grossly ignored. This ignorance is at the root of the confusion concerning the gifts of the Spirit. As noted earlier, everyone wants the power, but few want the process.

19

In John 3, Jesus commands us to be born again (born of the Spirit) and explains the process with notable detail. While the terms *born again* and *saved* are synonymous in the Christian vernacular, it's becoming evident that most folks misappropriate the term *saved* to propagate a false doctrine of an easy, powerless salvation—a "greasy grace" if you will. Jesus repeatedly condemned such wordplay and made it clear that "the road" to eternal life is so difficult that "few there be that find it" (Matt. 7:14).

The difficult road that Jesus speaks of is encapsulated by the born-again experience and the transforming process that follows. Jesus stated plainly, "he that shall endure unto the end, the same shall be saved" (Matt. 24:13). He isn't saying that the process itself can save us, but that the saved will always endure the process— "unto the end." If the born-again concept still confuses you, please refer to *Weapons of Our Warfare* for more discussion. In that book, I take a deeper look at the difference between born-again believers and those who merely claim to be Christians—the distance is as vast as heaven from hell (John chapter 3). We must be born again.

Baptism of the Holy Spirit and Fire

I've noticed that there is also some confusion in the body of Christ concerning the baptism of the Holy Spirit that Jesus promised at His ascension (Acts 1:5). To be specific, I've been asked whether this baptism is the same as the water baptism needed by all born-again believers. The short answer is no, as this is another example of dual meanings in some biblical terms, and it directly parallels the duality of the word *anointing*.

Before Jesus commanded us to be born again for salvation, John the Baptist prophesied the higher, God-given baptism, and herein we find the difference:

> I indeed baptize you with water unto repentance. but he that cometh after me is mightier than I, whose shoes I am not worthy to bear: he shall baptize you with the Holy Ghost, and with fire.
>
> —MATTHEW 3:11

Most of you already know that the Baptist denomination gets its name from John the Baptist, not vice versa. This particular John was the closest cousin of Jesus. He was called "the Baptist" because he was the most prolific baptizer in history, but he never baptized anyone with the Holy Spirit, nor can I.

Water baptism is the most important ceremony we can perform on this side of heaven, as it is our public declaration of our repentance and belief in Jesus as Lord and Savior, and it beautifully marks the beginning of the born-again life. I'm humbled that I've baptized more than twenty-five hundred people over the past year (praise God!), but when I baptize with water, I fully realize I'm not anointing anyone with the Holy Spirit.

However, God might be doing that at the very same time. It's a supernaturally palpable moment when He does, so I cherish my opportunities to feel His fire fall when I roll up my sleeves to baptize a believer in water. Tears flow every time!

As you might have surmised, the baptism of the Holy Spirit is another reference to the anointing. John the Baptist attaches the word *fire* to his baptism prophecy to remind us that we are being baptized with the consuming fire of God and to foreshadow the difficult process that always accompanies the born-again life.

God both empowers us for good works, and He refines us, forges us, and tests us "in the furnace of affliction" (Isa. 48:10). Through this prophecy, John the Baptist sheds light on the critical importance of the anointing in the life of a believer.

Power to Preach the Gospel

Moments before His ascension into heaven, Jesus promised that the baptism of the Holy Spirit was soon to come. He also made a direct connection between the power of the anointing and our ability to preach the gospel to all the world:

> And, being assembled together with them, commanded them that they should not depart from Jerusalem, but wait for the promise of the Father, which, saith he, ye have heard of me. For John truly baptized with water; but ye shall be baptized with the Holy Ghost not many days hence. When they therefore were come together, they asked of him, saying, Lord, wilt thou at this time restore again the kingdom to Israel? And he said unto them, It is not for you to know the times or the seasons, which the Father hath put in his own power. But ye shall receive power, after that the Holy Ghost is come upon you: and ye shall be witnesses unto me both in Jerusalem, and in all Judaea, and in Samaria, and unto the uttermost part of the earth.
>
> —ACTS 1:4–8

We now know the outpouring of the Holy Spirit and His fire began with the disciples who were present at Pentecost. If Jesus planned for the anointing to expire several centuries or even several decades before His return, I believe He would have noted that crucial twist in one of His *end times* discourses—but He didn't. Most theologians agree that the end times or last days began on Pentecost Sunday and continue through today. Two thousand years might seem like a long time to measure days, but to Jesus, a day is like a thousand years, and a thousand years is like a day (2 Pet. 3:8).

It Started at Pentecost

On that first Pentecost Sunday (which was also a major festival date on the Jewish calendar), 120 of Jesus' disciples were finally baptized with the Holy Spirit and fire. These freshly Spirit-filled disciples immediately left the Upper Room where the fire fell and walked out among the multitudes on the streets of Jerusalem to flow in their new anointing. The apostle Peter then boldly stepped into his destiny. The once fearful man, who had denied Jesus three times just seven weeks earlier, suddenly found his voice in the Spirit and quoted the prophet Joel to teach and prophesy:

> And it shall come to pass in the last days, saith God, I will pour out of my Spirit upon all flesh: and your sons and your daughters shall prophesy, and your young men shall see visions, and your old men shall dream dreams: And on my servants and on my handmaidens I will pour out in those days of my Spirit; and they shall prophesy.
>
> —ACTS 2:17–18

Three thousand new believers were added to their number that day. Along with the 120 core disciples, these were the first believers to be born again of the Spirit. With a mighty crescendo, Peter then prophesied that the *promise* of this gift was for *everyone* called by the Lord, "unto you, and to your children, and to all that are afar off," even as far off as you and me in the twenty-first century (Acts 2:38–41).

From that day forward, all who were born again began accessing the anointing. Peter and the others went on to heal the sick, prophesy, and perform "many wonders and signs" (Acts 2:43). They obeyed everything Jesus commanded them, and they preached the gospel in the face of great persecution wherever they went. Now it's our turn.

Greater Works Than These?

> Verily, verily, I say unto you, He that believeth on me, the works that I do shall he do also; and greater works than these shall he do; because I go unto my Father. And whatsoever ye shall ask in my name, that will I do, that the Father may be glorified in the Son. If ye shall ask any thing in my name, I will do it. If ye love me, keep my commandments. And I will pray the Father, and he shall give you another Comforter, that he may abide with you for ever.
>
> —JESUS (JOHN 14:12–16)

This verse gives us something to shout about! The Son of God gave us a promise that we'll do even greater works than He did! Jesus' words mean that we have the authority, the anointing, and the power to see more miracles and deliverance in people's lives than when Jesus walked the earth.

Now, some may wonder how that's possible. After all, Jesus was the Son of God, performing miracles left and right. But Jesus' earthly ministry was limited by time and space. He could only be in one place at a time. But when He ascended to heaven, He sent the Holy Spirit, the Comforter, to dwell within us, His followers.

Through the power of the Holy Spirit, we carry on the work of our Lord. That means we can lay hands on the sick and see them recover. We can cast out demons and set the oppressed free! We can speak the Word of God with boldness and see lives transformed by His mighty power. Yes, we can do greater works, my dear brothers and sisters.

Don't you dare doubt the power that resides in you. Believe the promise of Jesus, tap into the anointing of the Holy Spirit, and go out there, my friends, and do those greater works for the glory of God! The chains will be broken, the darkness will flee, and souls will be saved!

The promise is for us, so let us rise up in faith, ready to do those greater works and see the kingdom of God manifested here on earth. Let the power of Jesus flow through you as you bring deliverance to the captives. Let the world witness the mighty works of our Savior in and through us!

Keeping Things in Order

> For whatsoever things were written aforetime were written for our learning, that we through patience and comfort of the scriptures might have hope.
>
> —ROMANS 15:4

In my previous two books in this series, I fully explore how we are instructed to battle the devil and how to get our houses in order in these last days. If you've not yet read them, I strongly encourage you to do so as soon as possible, especially if you're not well-versed in spiritual warfare, according to the Bible.

Until you are equipped and trained in God's holy armor, the devil can twist your spiritual gifts to hurt others and destroy your calling. Sadly, we see a lot of that these days. Our Father in heaven is the God of order, so we must ensure we're standing on the firm foundations of biblical truth before we can righteously wield His sword and gifts with power.

> Not every one that saith unto me, Lord, Lord, shall enter into the kingdom of heaven; but he that doeth the will of my Father which is in heaven. Many will say to me in that day, Lord, Lord, have we not prophesied in thy name? and in thy name have cast out devils? and in thy name done many wonderful works? And then will I profess unto them, I never knew you: depart from me, ye that work iniquity.
>
> —JESUS (MATTHEW 7:21–23)

Iniquity is a KJV word for *lawlessness*. Many new believers rush to operate with supernatural power before understanding the Holy

Spirit or His consuming fire. The temptation to immediately access the anointing without proper understanding explains, in part, why the gifts are so easily abused and ignored. If you're familiar with the Marvel movies, you may recall that Iron Man's greatest strength was found in his power source, but he would have been easy prey without his suit of armor.

I know that can seem like a silly metaphor, but it works.

First things first. Make sure you suit up and boot up before you try to operate in your gifts out on the battlefield. Fools still rush in where wise men take time to prepare (Prov. 15:21), so don't be foolish about any of this.

Power to Move Mountains

> For verily I say unto you, That whosoever shall say unto this mountain, Be thou removed, and be thou cast into the sea; and shall not doubt in his heart, but shall believe that those things which he saith shall come to pass; he shall have whatsoever he saith.
>
> —JESUS (MARK 11:23)

I've witnessed many instances where someone accessed a spiritual gift in simple obedience, and an amazing work was done—in individuals and the church. In the famous verse above, Jesus tells us that the level of faith available to believers can indeed move mountains. These mountains are both literal and metaphorical. If you're discounting this concept or feel like you are reading some comic book stuff, you need to start taking the Bible more seriously.

Through my ongoing journey into the supernatural gifts of the Spirit, I'm finding that the more sensitive I am to the Holy Spirit, the more God reveals to me about people's lives. Suddenly I can walk up to folks and say things I would never have said. I know now that my former hesitation resulted from a lack of understanding, confidence, or both.

I'll soon talk more about this gift of knowledge. If you have it, don't get spooked. But if you hear things in your head that aren't edifying to the person in accordance with the Scripture, that's just kooky-spooky nonsense. It could be your imagination, but it may also be from the enemy. I believe this book will help you clear that up.

The Unction to Function

While we don't want to get ahead of God, we also don't want to hesitate when the Holy Spirit moves us. I recently taught a sermon at Global Vision that I titled *The Unction to Function*. With it, I taught how the anointing operates through us to inspire action and to give us knowledge about things we wouldn't otherwise know.

Unction is a KJV word that means anointing, so it makes sense that its modern connotations deal with a sudden boldness or inspiration. Like the word *anointing*, the word *unction* is also translated from the Greek word *charisma*.

> But ye have an unction from the Holy One, and ye know all
> things.
>
> —1 JOHN 2:20

Ultimately there is no prerequisite when God wants to use you. If God is moving you to act, you can trust that you'll know it's Him. It won't feel like a matter of your imagination or an idea of your own. When you get the holy unction to act, you won't want to risk missing God when He intends to use you to bless others. This underscores our absolute need to study the Bible, pray without ceasing, and remain continually connected with born-again believers. Through these, both confirmation and proper caution will come (Prov. 24:6).

Turning the Page

> For we are his workmanship, created in Christ Jesus unto good works, which God hath before ordained that we should walk in them.
>
> —EPHESIANS 2:10

Everyone has at least one gift, and some folks have a large mix. You don't have gifts because you're some sort of goody-two-shoes or have a great education. It's because God saw fit to give you that gift. He plans for you to reach people through your gifting—for the coming together of the body of Christ and the perfecting of the saints (Eph. 4:16).

The body can only experience revival and become unified, healthy, and whole when the eye, the ear, the mouth, the foot, the thumb, and the head are all working together. So, we all need to be a church that walks in the full power of the Holy Spirit and does good works.

Even with two seminary degrees, fifteen thousand sermons, and several books authored over my twenty-plus years as a revivalist and pastor, there are still many things in the Bible I don't fully understand. If you or your pastor think you have it all figured out, you're wrong. No one has mastered the book authored by God—the Creator of heaven and earth. That said, I pray the Lord eventually reveals all truth to me, and so should you.

There are matters of the kingdom of God and the born-again life that we must grow into over time, and I'm realizing and confessing that there are some areas where I've simply been wrong. I love you enough to humble myself to that truth so you can continue trusting the Holy Spirit's refining fire in me as He moves with power in my life. I praise God that the Bible has corrected me—not man, experience, or emotion. May we all stand corrected and teachable by the power of the living Word of God.

Seeing ye have purified your souls in obeying the truth through the Spirit unto unfeigned love of the brethren, see that ye love one another with a pure heart fervently: Being born again, not of corruptible seed, but of incorruptible, by the word of God, which liveth and abideth for ever.

—1 PETER 1:22–23

2

The Apostle Paul and the Gifts of the Spirit

I thank my God always on your behalf, for the grace of God
which is given you by Jesus Christ; That in every thing ye are
enriched by him, in all utterance, and in all knowledge; Even
as the testimony of Christ was confirmed in you: So that ye
come behind in no gift; waiting for the coming of our Lord
Jesus Christ: Who shall also confirm you unto the end, that
ye may be blameless in the day of our Lord Jesus Christ.
—1 CORINTHIANS 1:4–8

IF YOU READ verses 7 and 8 of that passage again, you'll notice
Paul writes, "ye come behind [lack] in no gift; waiting for the
coming of our Lord Jesus Christ: Who shall confirm you unto the
end." Knowing that this promise precedes his mention of the "perfect" event later in this letter should dismiss any lingering doubts
you may have about the continuation and perpetuation of the spiritual gifts.

Paul's first and second epistles (letters) to the church of Corinth probably could have been followed by a third epistle to the Corinthians because these people had a boatload of problems.

They were the most fall-down-the-steps immature people in the entirety of the New Testament, and the apostle Paul showed up in Corinth with his gospel Gatling gun blazing. He had to fix their theology and philosophy, and he couldn't do that with a BB gun.

The believers in Corinth didn't yet understand the end times and the return of Jesus, so Paul corrected them. They also struggled with their understanding of baptism, the Lord's Supper, all manners of sin, and of course, the truth about the spiritual gifts, so the Corinthians were a lot like the modern church. In fact, the Corinthians were doing virtually everything wrong.

There was even one cat in the church sleeping with his stepmother, and the people were nodding their heads and going along with it as if it was okay. Paul showed up on the scene, barrels blazing, and basically screamed, "You people are crazy! You need to church him up and deliver him over to Satan for the destruction of his flesh so that his spirit may be saved." (See 1 Corinthians 5:5.)

We find a wildly challenging set of chapters in these two epistles to the Corinthians, but God truly wanted these people to grow, just as He wants us to grow today. He knew they had lived for many years as spiritual babies—playing in a spiritual sandbox and sucking on a spiritual pacifier. So Paul said, "Look, I'm no longer gonna show up and change your diapers...you've got to move from milk to meat!"

As I explored in *Weapons of Our Warfare*, you can't just stay on the milk bottle all your spiritual life. You've got to be able to eat the meat of the Word of God, and you've got to be able to sink your teeth into it. Growth is not a suggestion; it is a command.

> But grow in grace, and in the knowledge of our Lord and
> Saviour Jesus Christ. To him be glory both now and for ever.
> Amen.
>
> —2 PETER 3:18

You're either growing or shrinking. You're either getting stronger
or weaker. And that applies to every aspect of your being. You're
never on neutral ground. You're either adding power and knowledge to your life or diminishing it. So we must *want* to grow, and
we must use the Word of God to accomplish that growth.

1 Corinthians Chapter 12

Through the message of *1 Corinthians 12*, the Lord uses Paul to
grow us up in our understanding of the spiritual gifts. He explains
how we can utilize the gifts of the Spirit in us, and he keeps it in
the context of the local church to ensure we remember the crucial
role of the body of Christ in the manifestation of the gifts.

While the Bible details the spiritual gifts in several places, this
particular chapter is most revealing. As discussed in the introduction, it's also the chapter on which the cessationist doctrine hangs,
so it's especially relevant to this study. Let's take a verse-by-verse
(expository) look at God's Word on these matters.

> Now concerning spiritual gifts, brethren, I would not have you
> ignorant.
>
> —1 CORINTHIANS 12:1

The spiritual gifts are not carnally gained (not through natural
learning or practice) but are spiritually given to those who are born
again. No one is born with spiritual gifts. The Holy Spirit alone
gives them to us. As discussed earlier, we are all born with good
gifts and talents, all given by God, but they lack supernatural power
until we have access to the anointing.

Even in the years that immediately followed the miracle-working life of Jesus, Paul recognized that 99 percent of the first-century church was ignorant of the existence and purpose of the spiritual gifts. By all indications, the body of Christ is no less ignorant two thousand years later. The gifts are either ignored or abused, and both paths have undermined their supernatural reality in our lives. For this, most believers are afraid to discuss the spiritual gifts despite their clear exposition in the Scriptures.

Let me shift gears and deliver a much-needed challenge to insecure folks and new Christians: Stop letting people talk you *out of* what the Holy Spirit has taught you *into*. Stop letting people tear you down when God Almighty is trying to build you up. Don't ever be afraid to experience and grow in something plainly taught in the Bible. The spiritual gifts are a supernatural reality, and the body of Christ cannot function correctly without them. Don't be ignorant to their need.

> Ye know that ye were Gentiles, carried away unto these dumb idols, even as ye were led.
> —1 CORINTHIANS 12:2

Sometimes people say I'm too confrontational in my sermons and writings. Yet, in this verse, I see Paul calling out folks for serving and following a bunch of "dumb idols." I love that. Today we see the church following a wide variety of dumb idols. While dumb means mute in this context, the term is indeed confrontational, but it's relatively mild compared to the harshest rebukes of Jesus and the prophets. When I compel you to stop believing and following the lies, deceptions, distractions, and other schemes of the enemy, I'm simply hoping to set you free from your dumb idols.

The Natural Desire for the Supernatural

Wherefore I give you to understand, that no man speaking by
the Spirit of God calleth Jesus accursed: and that no man can
say that Jesus is the Lord, but by the Holy Ghost.

—1 CORINTHIANS 12:3

Let me explain what's happening here in the historical context.
Paul was led to fully explain the spiritual gifts because the church
in Corinth was seeking supernatural power, but they were seeking
it in the wrong way. They were worshiping the idols of their culture
and false religions, believing that power and blessings flowed from
them. Simply put, they were practicing witchcraft, and they were
following heresies. Most of these people came from cultures where
sorcery and demonism were commonplace. Very little has changed.

All of us were born with a desire to engage with something bigger
and more powerful than us. Human beings have a natural desire
for spiritual encounters and supernatural power. This is why vam-
pire and witchcraft movies are so popular. People simply gravitate
toward that nonsense because they want to see something supernatural—right, wrong, or indifferent—because we are born with a
desire to witness mind-blowing power.

Some might be drawn to the occult out of curiosity or a desire
for control over their lives. But let me tell you, that's a dangerous
path to take. You might think you're gaining power, but what you're
really doing is opening doors to darkness and evil influences. And
engaging in witchcraft is like dancing with the devil himself. It's an
invitation for spiritual harm at any age, so don't be fooled by seem-
ingly harmless books and movies for kids that feature witches and
wizards. You can't play games with the devil and win. Witchcraft
and all occult influences you've opened yourself up to must be
commanded to go.

Those who venture into the occult or witchcraft are seeking

power and knowledge in all the wrong places. God has given us His Word as our guide. The devil tries to sway us with his counterfeits, but our strength comes from true power: the power of prayer, the power of the Word, and the power of the Holy Spirit.

So 1 Corinthians 12:3 says, in effect, "Oh, you want to see power? You've got to get in with the Holy Spirit first, and then you'll see some supernatural power." In the third verse of this rich chapter, Paul is basically saying that the only way you can truly proclaim that Jesus is Lord (and thereby be born again) is by the quickening power and inspiration of the Holy Spirit.

As Jesus said, "No man can come to me, except the Father which hath sent me draw him: and I will raise him up at the last day" (John 6:44). So the same Spirit of God that saves you is the same Spirit of God that gives you spiritual gifts. He is the only supernatural you want. He alone possesses the true supernatural power our souls crave.

We must be discerning, for there are many counterfeit powers and false promises in this world. But we need not chase after those illusions, for our God is the only true source of supernatural power that brings life, light, and genuine transformation.

Through the Holy Spirit, God equips us with spiritual gifts that are meant to build up the body of Christ. But it is essential that we use these gifts with humility, love, and in accordance with God's Word. We must seek His guidance and discernment to use these gifts for His purposes and not for selfish gain or personal glory.

Our focus should always remain on the Giver of these gifts, not the gifts themselves. They are meant to point us and others to the greatness and goodness of God. Let us not become enamored with the supernatural manifestations alone, but rather, let our hearts be filled with awe and gratitude for the One who imparts them.

Unity, Not Uniformity

> Now there are diversities of gifts, but the same Spirit.
>
> —1 CORINTHIANS 12:4

Through verse 4, we learn that the power in the gifts is not about the people but the Holy Spirit alone. The same Spirit that shows us that Jesus is Lord is the same Spirit that gives us these diverse gifts. It's important to note that God gives these for the sake of unity, not uniformity. Unity and uniformity are two very different things. We don't all dress the same, talk the same, look the same, spit the same, walk the same, or act the same—nor should we.

Many churches promote religious uniformity so effectively that everybody looks and acts alike. That's not a church—that's a cult. Unity results when you and I use our unique set of gifts for the glory of God in a way that results in the perfecting of the saints for the work of the ministry and the "building up" of the body of Christ (Eph. 4:12).

The gifts don't exist for you to look good or gain personal power. They exist so that Jesus can be more powerfully preached through you. They exist so that the church can become healthier and more unified.

Diversity and Differences

> And there are differences of administrations, but the same Lord. And there are diversities of operations, but it is the same God which worketh all in all.
>
> —1 CORINTHIANS 12:5–6

The gifts are given differently to every one of us, with broad-ranging diversity. From verses 5 and 6, we know that the gifts are diverse in their type, purpose, and recipients, and each presents a wide diversity of function, utilization, and intensity—in each church and each believer. So the gifts underscore the fact that you're not like me, and

I'm not like you. Wouldn't the world be burn-to-the-ground crazy if everybody was like Greg Locke? Wouldn't the world be boring if everybody was like you? We're all different, so we all administer our gifts in different ways, but it's always the same Spirit.

While God teaches the spiritual gifts in many ways throughout the Bible, Paul teaches them through three categories (perspectives)—manifestation, ministry, and motivation. Other Bible passages discuss the gifts in similar terms, but for simplicity, in this book, we'll focus on Paul's breakdown in 1 Corinthians chapter 12. Some gifts exist in multiple categories, and some, like miracles and helps, can represent many different gifts of a particular type. The various ways of categorizing and distinguishing the gifts are evidence of their wide diversity. All that said, don't let the semantics confuse you. I promise to avoid losing sight of the forest for the trees as we dive deeper into the anointing.

In verse 6, you'll see that Paul doubles down to ensure we understand the fundamentals of the origin and function of the gifts. God administers every single one of them and, in turn, fully operates every gift through us in diverse ways. If you study the Facebook world, you'll see that everybody is trying to be like somebody else. But if you study the Bible, you see that we're all supposed to be like Jesus while maintaining our diversity according to His Word.

Paul also reiterates that the Holy Spirit is the only source of power in the gifts. Please get comfortable with all the times I'll repeat that in this book, as God repeats it for good reason. When we're dealing with supernatural power, it's crucial that you stay mentally, physically, and spiritually connected to the Holy Spirit, or you'll risk falling into lawlessness and sorcery.

Likewise, every church standing for the truth of the gospel, on the fundamental realities of what the Bible teaches, is under the same God. The same God who powers Global Vision Bible Church powers every other living church, no matter how diverse we look and sound. The same Holy Spirit is bringing revival to every church that answers the call (1 Cor. 14:8), and He's working it all out "all in all" (1 Cor. 15:28).

The Manifestation of the Spirit

> But the manifestation of the Spirit is given to every man to profit withal.
>
> —1 CORINTHIANS 12:7

Don't be afraid of the word *manifestation*. God uses this word to describe the fruitful outworking of His Spirit through us. Here again, we are reminded of the main point. The gifts don't work through the manifestation of who you are, the manifestation of your boldness, or the manifestation of anything that you can control.

God alone manifests the gifts and decides which gifts we're each given. Through verse 7, we learn that the spiritual gifts benefit us— profit withal—when utilized in the Spirit. From here, Paul breaks down the nine gifts of 1 Corinthians 12 in a truly beautiful way.

> For to one is given by the Spirit the word of wisdom; to another the word of knowledge by the same Spirit.
>
> —1 CORINTHIANS 12:8

Notice the phrase "to another," as Paul is going to use it repeatedly. With it, Paul is pointing to the fact that everyone has at least one gift, and very few (if any) people will have all of them.

Those with a mixed bag of gifts will have one high-end gift that will work as a driving force for the others. More on that later.

Because we are all different, our capacity levels differ as well. God alone decides who among us has the capacity to properly handle each of the gifts. Like each gift itself, the capacity to operate in it— to the extent of its impact on an individual or the church—is not learned behavior, nor is it a matter of human genetics. It all flows from the Holy Spirit within. Each gift is God-created, God-given, God-anointed, and God-manifested.

> As every man hath received the gift, even so minister the same one to another, as good stewards of the manifold grace of God. If any man speak, let him speak as the oracles of God; if any man minister, let him do it as of the ability which God giveth: that God in all things may be glorified through Jesus Christ, to whom be praise and dominion for ever and ever. Amen.
>
> —1 PETER 4:10–11

3

The Gifts of Manifestation

*For to one is given by the Spirit the word of wisdom; to
another the word of knowledge by the same Spirit.*
—1 CORINTHIANS 12:8

A S WE CONTINUE to study Paul's 1 Corinthians 12 discourse, we
see wisdom is the first of these gifts. Many claim that wisdom
and a "word of knowledge" are the same thing, but they're unique
gifts. Likewise, the gift of wisdom is not a matter of education or
intelligence, so don't let these terms confuse you. Some folks have
the gift of wisdom far above others who have the same gift, and not
all have it to the same intensity. This is true of all the gifts. Godly
wisdom is the ability to decipher, deduce, and determine the correct biblical answer in a given situation.

As noted earlier, though the outpouring of the gifts and widespread indwelling of the Holy Spirit are post-ascension phenomena,
God has been anointing select people with His Spirit and His gifts
from the beginning, and King Solomon is a profound example.

41

Solomon wielded wisdom with world-changing fruitfulness while he walked in God's righteousness, but sadly, his eventual severe disobedience and idolatry upended him later in life.

When Solomon's wisdom waned, it wasn't because his IQ took a nosedive. Solomon lost his godly wisdom because he lost sight of God and stopped standing on the Word of God. Tragically, he was "carried away unto these dumb idols" (1 Cor. 12:2), and his failure to operate in his God-given wisdom brought destruction to Israel. All of us need to learn from Solomon's fall.

Some believers are so gifted with godly wisdom that they can walk into your life and—like young Solomon—give you startling wisdom about a present situation. That prospect can spook some folks, but it shouldn't. The Bible compels us to want greater wisdom, for as long as it stands on the Word of God, it can only profit the body of Christ (Jas. 1:5). I don't know about you, but I spent far too much of my life hanging out with stupid folks and chasing dumb idols. I'm done with it. I want to surround myself with people gifted with wisdom for the rest of my life.

Word of Knowledge?

On the back half of verse 8 of Paul's discourse, we see, "to another a word of knowledge." This particular gift makes people especially nervous. You might be thinking, "Word of knowledge? Oh my goodness! That sounds so spooky. What does that mean?"

It means exactly what the Bible says it means. God gives some people spiritual insight into other people's lives, and—if it's a legitimate gift of God—this insight will not contradict the Word of God or the revealed will of God. People with this gift simply have knowledge given to them by God and God alone. This isn't crystal-ball fortune-teller nonsense. It's a spiritual gift.

We often hear people talk about women's intuition. While I believe that's a natural gift from God, it's not what we're discussing here. This sort of intuition is God-given knowledge, where someone can tell you truths they had no way of knowing through natural means. But this caveat must be repeated—a word of knowledge will never contradict the Bible. If someone gives you "a word" that goes against the Scripture, it's not a word of knowledge but a word from hell (demonically inspired).

However, if it lines up with the revealed truth of the Bible, it should not be ignored.

Now, I'm not claiming to have this gift, but during the time leading up to my decision to write this book, God downloaded knowledge into my spirit that I had no reason to know outside of Him. There have been things I've said from the pulpit, in a prayer meeting, or in a meet-and-greet line that I had no reason to know, yet it proved to be 100 percent true.

A Simple Example of a "Word"

I was recently preaching in a little-bitty tent in Somerset, Kentucky, and the place was packed. I was preaching on the call of Jeremiah in the Book of Jeremiah chapter 1 when I stopped right in the middle of my message and stepped down from the platform to walk amongst the folks I was preaching to.

On this night, something kept bubbling up in my spirit, and I knew the Holy Spirit was compelling me to say something. I was hesitant at first because I had never been that sort of preacher, but on this occasion, it was like I couldn't even stop myself. I walked up about two feet from this young man in the crowd and looked him straight in the eye, and with zero forethought and very little hesitation, I said to him:

> I don't even know who you are, sir, but I'm gonna tell you
> something right now. God's got a special anointing on your
> life and people have been trying to talk you out of what
> the Holy Ghost has talked you into. God tells me you're a

> Jeremiah, that you've got a calling on you, that you have a
> ministry equipping in you, and that people are trying to stop
> you. You have got to stop what you're doing and start living
> up to what God has placed in you. You must believe that you
> have great gospel value.

His eyes bugged clear out of his head like two Jimmy Dean sausage patties, and it was like a dam just broke inside him. He cried and cried. As soon as I released that word, I immediately went back to my preaching and didn't think anything else of it—other than I thought it was weird.

When I finished the message, I gave the pastor the microphone and walked to the table where I'd be signing books and hugging necks. As I walked, it occurred to me that I've always thought these things were embarrassingly unbiblical, but I was wrong. In the past, I would have fought off that *unction*, but now I realize I was only snuffing out the Holy Spirit's fire in me and thereby failing God (1 Thess. 5:19). Had I done that on this occasion, I would have cheated that young man of all God wanted to do in him that night.

When the Holy Spirit manifests supernaturally through us, we must let Him have His way—especially if it strips our pride.

That's one of the ways the gift blesses us for our obedience. The use of our gifts can change the trajectory of someone's life. I am sure that it changed this cat's life forever. I'm positive that he'll never forget it, and if he ever starts to go back to the nonsense of his old ways and leaves what he knows God *unctioned* him to do on that fateful night, he's going to remember this little hillbilly who stood two feet in front of him and called him out in front of the people of God.

It Has Always Been There

As I admitted above, I have always had these impressions. I just didn't know what to do with them—except when I could work them into my counseling. But today I know I must share them as a gift of the Spirit—a word of knowledge from the Lord—not a word from Greg. That was a big leap for a former cessationist like me.

I'm finally ready to embrace it as a gift intended for the benefit of others, and I'm starting to let the Holy Spirit flow in and through me. I'm starting to understand exactly when the Lord wants me to say something that He spoke into me, and I'm starting to recognize the unction to function in the Spirit. If it's from God, it will always benefit the hearer, so we all need to let it flow. It's a beautiful transaction that grows and inspires everyone involved.

Having said that, we must recognize that sometimes the knowledge can sting, but we can't let that deter us. If it's from God, it will still benefit the hearer. Here's an example from my own life. Recently, a dear friend in the ministry was able to give me details about my childhood that only God could have revealed to him. Sharing this word of knowledge led to a dramatic healing in my heart and mind that I needed more than I could have ever realized before that night. My friend has this gift, and he blessed me greatly with it, as I have felt delivered and healed of that wounding ever since. So don't shy away from folks with this gift. God knows what you truly need for a breakthrough, and He wants to give it to you, so fear not.

Water-Walking Faith

> To another faith by the same Spirit; to another the gifts of healing by the same Spirit.
>
> —1 CORINTHIANS 12:9

To be born again, we all must have faith to some degree, but some people have an overflow far beyond the faith that saves. Some folks have water-walking faith. Some have mountain-moving faith. Some have a "God's going to pay my bills down to the last dollar" sort of faith—and that's a gift. This sort of faith is at such magnitude that we can only marvel. I want to operate in that gift.

Of course, without faith, it's impossible to please God (Heb. 11:6), so we all need to have the faith that saves us since faith is the very thing that takes us from earth to heaven. But as I discussed at great length in *Weapons of Our Warfare*, we also need to actively grow our faith on a day-by-day, hour-by-hour basis. Folks with this great gift inspire us to want more faith.

When we meet people with this gift, we must realize that it's not their faith in and of itself that empowers them to have increased measures of that faith. The object of their faith alone gives the gift and makes it operate properly—God alone. If I were to have faith in the force of gravity to keep me grounded, I would get what gravity can do. But when I have faith in a Holy God, I get what a Holy God can do, and He can do exceedingly, abundantly more than we can ever ask or think (Eph. 3:20).

If you have this gift, you are able to believe God for the impossible things, and that's contagious. The modern church desperately needs more of you to recognize what you have and start walking in it to fulfill your calling in the body of Christ. As is true of all the gifts, though faith manifests with unique and diverse intensity in each person, it is still powered by "the same Spirit." Be sure to notice in Paul's discourse that Spirit is written with a capital S, denoting the Holy Spirit of God. When you see that, be reminded that we're not talking about the common word *spirit*, we're talking about God.

The Gift of Healing

In the back half of verse 9, we read, "To another the gifts of healing by the same Spirit." This may be the most controversial gift of them all. The gift of healing has been counterfeited to disgusting degrees ever since the days of Paul, and it continues today.

Let me tell you why I (and so many cessationists) have had such an aversion to the gift of healing. It's because it has been abused for many generations and brought so much ridicule upon the body of Christ that even non-cessationists tend to shy away from folks who claim this gift. For that, most folks with this gift simply ignore it despite the never-ending need for healing in the church and the world.

God tells us that He forgives all our iniquities and heals all our diseases (Ps. 103:3). Be reminded that He never revoked this amazing promise—on the contrary. Healing is still something that God does miraculously and supernaturally to display His glory, and He still uses those with this beautiful gift to bring healing to all people in all nations. It's an example and clear proof of what Jesus meant when He said we could do even "greater works" during these last days than we see Him perform in the Gospels (John 14:12). Where Jesus healed multitudes as a man during the first century, He is ready to heal billions through His Holy Spirit today, but folks with this gift must be His hands and feet in this regard.

Jesus' final discourse in the garden (John 14–17) was His most supernatural, encouraging, empowering, everlasting, Holy Spirit-packed teaching in the entire Bible, and cessationism has castrated it with disastrous results. You might have noticed that I have cited that discourse numerous times in this book.

This sort of powerless, lukewarm thinking (Rev. 3:16) has made the Western church dry as cracker juice and lifeless as dead men's bones. We desperately need to wake them up to the truth.

I pray the body of Christ comes to such a place of understanding that everything God says is yes and amen—for His glory (2 Cor. 1:20). As a great preacher of yesteryear said, "May the Lamb that was slain receive the reward of His suffering." Jesus did not die so we could lie in sickness and walk in misery. He came to give us life and life more abundantly (John 10:10). The current explosion of hypochondria (the spirit of infirmity, Luke 13:11) might never have touched the church if the people of God with the gift of healing were obedient.

My Hands, Tai's Back

Do I believe in the gift of supernatural healing in a believer? Yes, I absolutely do, but I used to disbelieve. I would never have admitted that online because I didn't want the hate mail, but it's true. Today I would rather get those letters than fail God. Yes, it must be done in order, but the Bible says it's still an active gift for very good reason, so we need to get over ourselves and get right with God.

So, whether I have this particular gift or not is yet to be discovered. I hope I have it. I hope you have it too. I believe healing ministry is a calling on our body at Global Vision, so I'm expecting to soon see folks with this anointing raising their hands to answer their calling. This belief isn't just wishful thinking; it was born from a "suddenly" that helped start me on this journey into the supernatural of God.

My wife, Tai, has scoliosis (curvature of the spine) in a bad way. Her spine looks like a West Virginia road where you can see someone's headlights and taillights at the same time as they come around a turn. About two months ago, she was snoozing after having experienced a nearly debilitating day of back pain. She has endured chronic pain from scoliosis as long as I've known her, and her flare-ups can be gut-wrenching.

As I watched her sleep that night, I thought, "Hmm. She's asleep. I can't make that much of a fool out of myself. I don't have a microphone; no one is watching, so why not?" I laid down on my side right next to her and gently put my hand on her back. Then I said:

Lord, I'm nothing special, but I don't have anything to lose by asking. It's the middle of the night, and it's just me, You, and her in the room, so Lord, I pray in the mighty name of Jesus that my wife's back will straighten up because I've read in Your Word that You have touched others and Your power came upon them, and You straightened them up. I read about a man who, for thirty-eight years, couldn't even walk, and the Bible says that his ankle bones came together, and he stood up, walked, and leaped, and praised God. Would You do that for my wife?

I didn't get too loud in the room so as not to embarrass myself if she woke up. I didn't know what I was doing; it was the first time I had ever attempted to believe that God might answer that sort of prayer. So I decided not to tell her; I just closed out my prayer and hoped for the best. I simply waited.

A few days passed, and we were driving down the road when she said, "Can I ask you a question?"

And I said, "I reckon."

She said, "Did you lay hands on my back and pray for me?"

And I said, "Yes, ma'am, I did. Are you worse?"

And she said, "You're going to think I'm crazy."

I said, "No, I'm not, or I wouldn't have done it."

Finally, she said, "I haven't had an ounce of pain in my back since that night I struggled. I'm telling you, I felt a shift when I got up the next morning."

There was a time when I would have heard a story like that and said, "That's the dumbest nonsense I've ever heard!" But this was nothing like any of that. As the old adage goes, we must stop throwing out the baby with the bathwater. God is birthing something miraculous in all of us. We need only believe.

My Aversion to Strange Fire

> And Nadab and Abihu, the sons of Aaron, took either of them his censer, and put fire therein, and put incense thereon, and offered strange fire before the LORD, which he commanded them not.
>
> —LEVITICUS 10:1

The devil can't create, so he imitates and counterfeits. He does this not just to cause confusion but to cause such deep division that we develop a hatred and aversion to the real thing—he keeps us from the real thing by accentuating the wrong thing. We've sometimes seen the wrong thing in the American church, so we're automatically skeptical when we see the real thing. The gift of healing is strange to those of us who were raised Baptist or under one of the other cessationist denominations because we've never seen it in action in our churches. So, if you still feel that way, I get it.

When I'd see people fall over or claim they were healed on television or in videos, I used to say, "Well, those people are just emotionally unstable and easy to manipulate." I thought I was wise to those frauds who put hot peppers on their hands and asked, "Oooh...do you feel that heat?" Back then, I said things like, "Yeah! You put chili pepper on their face! They'll feel some heat when you pull that parlor trick, you con man!" You can google me and find videos where I said tough things about some well-known healing ministries. So I understand the aversion. I've lived in it most of my life. But we all must get past that scheme of the enemy.

The Real Thing

Nothing about the spiritual gifts is natural or normal to my wife and me. I came up hard-core Baptist, and she came out of a ditch of addiction. This is all very different to us. The first time I saw someone fall out during a healing service at Global Vision, you'd better believe I got uncomfortable fast. I was like, "Whaaaaat is that? Don't they know I was raised a Baptist, and we just don't do that? Would they please just hurry up?"

I got as nervous as a long-tail cat in a room full of rocking chairs. But I could also discern that it was ushered in by the Holy Spirit and aligned with the truth in the Bible. For that, it didn't take long for me to see the beauty of all God was doing in me and our church.

Sometime later, I was preaching in a Baptist church where they knew of my Baptist roots, and I said, "You know, the Bible says, 'When I became a man, I put away childish things.'" I thought it would be good comic relief, but nobody laughed, nobody said amen, and nobody clapped, even though I was just joking—sort of.

I had been rejecting the concept of supernatural healing from the word go. But then I watched it happen in the privacy of my bedroom, the sanctity of my home church, and the many other places since that night with Tai. I've finally watched it happen with my own eyes, and I know when I'm seeing the real thing.

Do you know how they train bank tellers to identify counterfeit money? They don't get them to study the fake stuff; they teach them how to intimately know the characteristics of the real thing. The same should be true concerning spiritual gifts. Stop fixating on the frauds and look to the Word of God.

Trusting It All to Him

If God is calling me out as one with the gift of healing for the masses, we'll find out soon enough. I get enough exposure to hurting people. But if it's a gift just strong enough in me to help my wife and my kids get healed, I'm all in for that too. God's will be done. We all have power in our prayer, so if that's the extent of my gifting in this regard, I'll still be grateful. Whatever God has for me, I'll be sure to use it faithfully at every opportunity.

I'm finally going to believe what the Bible says about the gifts and start to boldly operate in the ones that God has for me, whichever they may be, to whatever degree they may come. I believe someone out there has the anointing so strong that they can heal terminal cancer.

Doesn't that sound like something God wants for us? You can either believe in His power or wallow in your weakness. You can't do both.

As we turn to the next chapter to continue our expository study of the gifts in 1 Corinthians, be encouraged by these promises of God:

> Be careful for nothing; but in every thing by prayer and supplication with thanksgiving let your requests be made known unto God. And the peace of God, which passeth all understanding, shall keep your hearts and minds through Christ Jesus. Finally, brethren, whatsoever things are true, whatsoever things are honest, whatsoever things are just, whatsoever things are pure, whatsoever things are lovely, whatsoever things are of good report; if there be any virtue, and if there be any praise, think on these things. Those things, which ye have both learned, and received, and heard, and seen in me, do: and the God of peace shall be with you.
>
> —PHILIPPIANS 4:6–9

4

Do Miracles Still Happen?

To another the working of miracles; to another prophecy;
to another discerning of spirits; to another divers kinds
of tongues; to another the interpretation of tongues.
—1 CORINTHIANS 12:10

A S WE CONTINUE our verse-by-verse expository study of 1 Corinthians chapter 12, Paul starts verse 10 with the phrase, "To
another the working of miracles." In this context, Paul is not super
specific concerning exactly what the workings of the miracles are,
but we can fully trust that some people have been given an extra
measure of faith to work miracles (1 Cor. 12:9). Miracles are hap-
penings that would be deemed scientifically or even supernaturally
impossible absent the intervention of our omnipotent, omniscient,
omnipresent God.

Men have watered down the word *miracle* over the centuries, so
let's be sure to give that word its full power. It is not a miracle when
your kids clean their rooms. It's not a miracle when your favorite

team suddenly wins a game they should have lost. Real miracles are acts of God that require the power of God, so we should be more careful how we use that word.

The Bible teaches us that demons still flee by the power of Jesus' name. This type of miracle is especially relevant today (Mark 16:17; Acts 19:13). The power of God has not diminished, and He desires to set the captives free. As believers in Jesus, when we proclaim His name with faith, we tap into that supernatural power that can drive out demons and witness the same miraculous acts of deliverance today that we read about in the Bible.

We have all met people and will continue to meet people under demonic possession. If you don't believe that, you don't believe the Bible. Throughout the Scriptures, we see Jesus casting out demons with a simple command. His authority was undeniable, and even the forces of darkness recognized His power. And here's the beautiful truth, my friend: Jesus has given us the privilege and authority to use His name to overcome evil and set the captives free!

We could talk endlessly about all the types and examples of miracles performed in the Bible, especially those worked by Jesus while He walked the earth as a man. All of these are miraculously possible through the prayers and actions of men and women of God who are gifted with this particular anointing.

Miracles to Witness His Glory

> God also bearing them witness, both with signs and wonders, and with divers miracles, and gifts of the Holy Ghost, according to his own will?
>
> —HEBREWS 2:4

This is another topic that many, both inside and outside the church, have developed an instant aversion to, and for good reason. A miracle is to be a supernatural display of the power of God, not a show! As the Book of Hebrews shows, God performs "signs and wonders" and "divers miracles" through the anointed to serve, "bearing them witness" to His glory.

When the person performing the miracles becomes the central character, or when the miracle becomes a spectacle rather than a sign and wonder to witness God's glory, it is out of order. In these cases, there is a wrong motivation behind utilizing the gift. It is lawlessness when it puts the spotlight on people instead of Jesus.

Do I hope to discover that God wants to work miracles through me and many others in the church? I absolutely do. But I'm not so anxious to see the real thing that I'd ever condone the counterfeit. There must be no "fake it till I make it" in the body of Christ. If it's not the real thing, it's demonic, so let's make sure we're approaching all the gifts with proper awe and reverence to God.

Do Prophets Still Exist?

> To another the working of miracles; to another prophecy; to another discerning of spirits; to another divers kinds of tongues; to another the interpretation of tongues.
> —1 CORINTHIANS 12:10

Continuing with verse 10 of Paul's discourse, we see that God gives "to another prophecy." Here is where things have really gone off the rails for cessationist denominations, as most believe that prophets and prophecy are for the Old Testament alone. But, as we say in the South, "That dog hunts," whether you read the Bible or not. As we proved in the introduction, both are still very biblical, and even unbelievers have seen it proven across history and to this day.

In this letter, Paul is speaking to the church about having prophets in the body of the New Testament church going forward, not about Old Testament history. We see proof of that if we jump further down in 1 Corinthians 12.

> And God hath set some in the church, first apostles, second-
> arily prophets, thirdly teachers, after that miracles, then gifts
> of healings, helps, governments, diversities of tongues.
> —1 CORINTHIANS 12:28

From this, we know that some people have a unique discerning ability to speak prophetically within the context of the local church. You can be sure that if it is a legitimate gift from God, it will always operate within the context of the Bible, so we should never shy away from the real thing.

Prophecy in Action

All of this is extraordinarily liberating for me to say because a couple of years ago, I would have denied the reality of ongoing prophecy. But how can we deny this truth when the Bible talks so clearly about the role of prophets and prophecy without ever saying they would cease before Jesus returns? We can't.

Paul helps us to understand that some people in the church have the uncanny ability to see the direction that things are going within a particular context. From there, they are responsible for ensuring this impression lines up with the Bible through study and prayer and then delivering it to the church or relevant individual as a "word." This is the gift of prophecy.

If you or anyone you know ever says, "I know the Bible says this, but the Holy Spirit is telling me something entirely different," to that, I say, "Wrongo, bucko!" The Holy Ghost and the Holy Bible are now and will always be unified and free of contradiction. God will never tell you to do something that the Bible definitively speaks against.

Someone with this gift will never take the Word of God and manipulate, twist, or spin its context. If someone says, "I've just got this feeling," but it doesn't harmonize with the Holy Scripture, it's not a prophetic impression. It's heartburn or worse. That's where prophetic discernment comes into play. So those who believe that they have this gift need to take great care to get trained in its proper operation.

The Discerning of Spirits

As we return to verse 10 of Paul's discourse, we see, "to another," God gifts the "discerning of spirits." Notice that the word *spirits* is in plural form. I need to remind you that we are in a war, and in this war, we must arm ourselves with the knowledge and discernment that multiple spirits are at work in this world. This is the reason the apostle John tells us:

> Beloved, believe not every spirit, but try the spirits whether they are of God: because many false prophets are gone out into the world.
>
> —1 JOHN 4:1

If we could cut into the heavenly realm right now and look around at what's going on, we would see principalities, powers, and spiritual wickedness in high places at work everywhere we look (Eph. 6:12). We would see angels and demons fighting it out in the air and on the ground all around us.

People with the gift of discernment don't necessarily see the spiritual realm, but they are empowered to perceive the root causes of spiritual issues. The gift of discernment allows people to rightly identify and understand spiritual dynamics at work in a person's life. This gift grants insight into whether a person is being oppressed, influenced, or tormented by demonic forces. Those with this gift can differentiate between the working of the Holy Spirit, the human spirit, and demonic spirits, which helps them determine the root causes of spiritual issues, identifying strongholds, and guiding the appropriate course of action for deliverance.

We all need to train our spiritual eyes, and some are especially gifted in this area. Discerning these spirits is relatively easy for those with this gift, but the rest of us must pay closer attention to gain similar awareness.

Believers should always expect God's fresh, legitimate fire to spark in and around us. But as discussed in the previous chapter, counterfeit fire is also everywhere. When we recognize or discern it, we must call it out. When it doesn't line up with the gospel and God's teachings to the New Testament church, we have to junk it.

Suspicion vs. Discernment

We also must make sure that we are not confusing suspicion with discernment. They can appear and even feel similar if you're not careful. Some will say, "Well, I discerned that from the Lord," or, again, "I have a feeling in my spirit," but if their judgment is cloudy or skewed by some sort of selfish interest, they'll be operating in unholy suspicion. If you have a true ability to discern spirits through the operation of the Holy Spirit, you will know it, as with the gift of knowledge and the gift of prophecy.

People with the gift of discernment have a unique ability to know the direction that the Spirit of God is flowing and are in such close connection with the Spirit within that they know what is going on or soon to come in the spiritual realm—and thereby what might soon happen in the natural.

As a word of caution, people with this gift and those with the gift of knowledge and the gift of prophecy can often look like "jerks for Jesus" because these are not passive, quiet gifts. On the contrary, someone with these gifts cannot just sit silently on vital information delivered to them by God that contains a warning or divine advice.

What good would come if the Holy Spirit convinced them of something evil, wicked, or nefarious afoot, but they stayed silent to keep the peace? We are to be peacemakers, not peacekeepers (Matt. 5:9; 10:34). There can be no real peace if we try to keep it through fear of upsetting folks that need to know the truth. For this reason, God gives a higher level of boldness to folks with gifts that are prophetic in nature—especially the discerning of spirits.

They Shall Speak With New Tongues

> And these signs shall follow them that believe; In my name shall they cast out devils; they shall speak with new tongues.
>
> —JESUS (MARK 16:17)

When Jesus says there are signs that mark the born again, we should want them, not dread them. As we continue our study of Paul's gifts discourse where we left off, he finally broaches the awkward question. Tongues? Really? Referring to verse 10, Paul writes, "to another divers [various] kinds of tongues," and he continues, "to another the interpretation of tongues" (1 Cor. 12:10).

"Tongues" is another of the more controversial subjects in the church. Raised a Baptist, I get that, and I had to personally deal with it. Tongues are syllabic utterances of no known meaning to the speaker that sound a lot like an actual language. These utterances can be a known foreign language, but it would have to be unknown to the speaker to constitute the gift of tongues. Tongues are spoken for various reasons but are always exclusively spoken or prayed to God, and only the Holy Spirit can interpret them.

> For he that speaketh in an unknown tongue speaketh not unto men, but unto God: for no man understandeth him; howbeit in the spirit he speaketh mysteries.
>
> —1 CORINTHIANS 14:2

It's important to know that this gifting has two types of tongues. First, there is the manifested gift of speaking in tongues. This type is purely prophetic, it's common to public gatherings or group settings like the local church, and it requires someone with the gift of interpretation to interpret. This is the only form of tongues that requires an interpreter.

Second, there is the manifested gift of praying in tongues (also called a prayer language) within your personal prayer closet, which is metaphorical for your inner secret place, where you communicate one-on-one with God and no one else (Matt. 6:6). The privacy of your prayer closet is especially important when you're praying in tongues.

This secret place can indeed be a physical space like an actual closet, but it's really just a state of spiritual focus where you get alone with God and shut everything else out—anywhere at any time—even if you're around people in a church or out in public.

As is true with all prayer, you must know that you are praying to an audience of One. When I pray in my secret place, I'm glad to know God understands Tennessee Hillbilly, but He doesn't have to if I'm praying in tongues. He understands every utterance when you're sincerely praying in your prayer language because—as is true for all the gifts—tongues flow from the Holy Spirit within.

When someone publicly speaks in tongues, the person interpreting will receive the interpretation directly from God as a gift. Speaking in tongues is a prophetic act that requires a separate interpreter, as the speaker cannot interpret their own spoken tongue, so we must take great care to ensure it is properly administered. Paul addresses proper order in his letter to the Corinthians:

> If any man speak in an unknown tongue, let it be by two, or at the most by three, and that by course; and let one interpret.

> But if there be no interpreter, let him keep silence in the church; and let him speak to himself, and to God.
> —1 CORINTHIANS 14:27–28

This makes sense to me. What good is a bunch of meaningless utterances or the sudden use of a foreign language if no one understands it? If it's from God and for God, it will be accompanied by an interpretation that edifies the people and, thereby, edifies the church. Yes, these gifts can easily be counterfeited, and that's why we need to discuss these matters in our churches. But born-again believers can generally discern the real from the fake when the real thing flows. People can be afraid of speaking in tongues because it has been so badly confused and comingled with praying in tongues, but it really isn't that complicated.

My Firsthand Experience

I went out recently with a dear friend to a men's gathering in the Thompson's Station area, south of Nashville. It looked like one of our Monday morning Bible studies with the men at Global Vision, jam-packed with forty or fifty men of prayer. It was a very informal gathering that I attended, pretty much incognito. I didn't know how many might have seen me online or might have known my name, and honestly, I didn't care. They all eventually knew I was a pastor, so I hoped for something to flow through them that would encourage me.

I wasn't there to speak or operate as a pastor in any way. I was there because I was told I could get ministered to by folks with the anointing. I realize now that I need that more than ever, and so do you. As I was sitting there, one of the guys got up and said, "Hey, Pastor Locke, can we pray over you?"

I said, "Absolutely, you can pray over me," and moved to sit in a chair where many could gather around me.

Soon after they all started praying for me, this one guy looked straight at me and said, "You've got the spirit of a lion, and you need to roar louder than you've ever roared because they're about to come against you and attack you like never before." Not exactly something I wanted to hear. At that time, I had no inkling that Congress would soon put me on their hit list for preaching in Washington, DC, on January 6, and the media craziness had not yet exploded, so I didn't have any reason to believe he was right, yet somehow I knew he was.

At that moment, I was thinking, "How does this guy know this, and why would he say that? Does he know me better than I think?" Then someone prayed, "Lord, I just feel like this guy has the spirit of John the Baptist. Lord, give him courage, give him courage, give him courage." Then someone prayed, "Oh my Lord, bless this man, fill this man, bless his church, protect his church, protect them, protect them." They just kept praying and praying for protection.

All the while, there was a guy in front of me, down on his knees, weeping. He had his hands clasped around mine as they all prayed. The sincerity and intensity of their prayers were beyond powerful. This wasn't just a bunch of guys trying to pray to act spiritual. These men were gifted in the Spirit.

By this time, I was crying like a baby. Suddenly it got quiet, and the guy weeping on his knees started praying in what sounded like Swahili but wasn't. He went on like this for a short while. Once he finished, before anyone else could start praying, another guy suddenly said, "I have an interpretation from God." I was just mesmerized. What he said was remarkable and has already proven prophetic. Likewise, the man who spoke the tongue was moved by the interpretation, so there was agreement in the Spirit across the board.

That unprecedented experience was beautiful and beautifully encouraging. It all occurred in proper order according to the Word of God, and for that reason, none of it freaked me out as it would have not too long ago. It was anointed, and I finally got it.

Oneness in Christ

> But all these worketh that one and the selfsame Spirit, dividing to every man severally as he will. For as the body is one, and hath many members, and all the members of that one body, being many, are one body: so also is Christ. For by one Spirit are we all baptized into one body, whether we be Jews or Gentiles, whether we be bond or free; and have been all made to drink into one Spirit.
>
> —1 CORINTHIANS 12:11–13

Across the next three verses of Paul's discourse, we see a recurring theme of unity through the Spirit, in Christ—one and the selfsame. The purpose of the church isn't the unity of mankind; it's our spiritual oneness in Christ, through the same Spirit, no matter who we are. In this passage, we see, "one and the selfsame Spirit… one body…by one Spirit…baptized into one body…made to drink into one Spirit." Nothing creates unity more powerfully than the anointing of the Holy Spirit—according to His will—and His will is unity in the Spirit.

In writing that we "drink of one Spirit," Paul reminds us of our power source and life force as we live in unity in the body of Christ—God alone. For me, that also speaks to the purity of His character and His emotional self-control placed in us. You cannot have the Spirit of God without emotion, but you can easily have emotion without the Spirit of God. Don't miss that. It's crucial that you get it.

We must ensure we don't go off the rocker as we move, swinging too far to one extreme or the another (Eccles. 7:18). When you operate in your gifting, remember to model yourself after Jesus. Ensure you approach every situation with Him in your mind, heart, soul, and strength, no matter where you come from. Seek His emotional dispositions no matter who you are or what you do.

Embracing Diversity in Unity

> For the body is not one member, but many. If the foot shall say, Because I am not the hand, I am not of the body; is it therefore not of the body?
>
> —1 CORINTHIANS 12:14–15

In this interesting pair of verses, Paul basically asks us a rhetorical question that can be answered with a resounding *yes*. Is the foot part of the body, even if it isn't as popular as the hand? Of course, it is. If you chop off a foot, the hand is going to suffer. If you chop off a hand, the foot is going to suffer. Individual prominence and purpose are irrelevant in the body of Christ, for we are *one* as God is *one* (John 17:11). God designs the different parts of our bodies to complement each other, and He designs us the same way.

In the body of Christ, we are not in competition; we are in cooperation. Metaphorically speaking, it's foolish for the foot to argue with the hand. While they have entirely different functions, they only thrive when they work together for the body as a whole. The same is true for us.

> And if the ear shall say, Because I am not the eye, I am not of the body; is it therefore not of the body? If the whole body were an eye, where were the hearing? If the whole were hearing, where were the smelling?
>
> —1 CORINTHIANS 12:16–17

If the whole body was just a mass of eyes, we wouldn't just look creepy; we wouldn't even be able to function or feed ourselves. As simplistic as that sounds, it's the point God is making here. Look around you and notice how much everyone is comparing themselves to others, envying others for what they have, and wishing they could be like them.

Some are thinking, "I'm not valuable around here. I'm just an awkward ear, and all I can do is hear," or, "I'm just an eyeball... what good is seeing if I don't do what the other senses can do?" That is a huge part of the problem in the church. We haven't learned the value of our individual anointing nor how to properly team up with others as they operate in theirs. It's so seldom seen that it can sound unrealistic, yet God commands it, so we know it's non-negotiable.

It's About the Body

> But now hath God set the members every one of them in the body, as it hath pleased him. And if they were all one member, where were the body? But now are they many members, yet but one body.
>
> —1 CORINTHIANS 12:18–20

Sometimes we read or hear terms like *body of Christ* and brush them off as outmoded religious jargon. I believe God's body metaphor has been among the most ignored, as it reveals why the modern church has become so divided and powerless. Unity is an uncomfortable teaching in this selfish, "me first" world. Meanwhile, the actual body of Christ—the remnant church of born-again believers—is rising up through the power of the Holy Spirit anointing (Rom. 11:5), so fear not. Being the remnant, or "elect" as Jesus called us, though we are assured victory in the end, we must remember that this rescue mission isn't about us. Jesus commanded us to fulfill the Great Commission and to seek and save the lost (Luke 19:10). That command applies to the masses of unregenerate Christians in the dying modern church.

God doesn't give us gifts and place them in the body of Christ to please us, our families, the world, or the culture, so we need to get over ourselves. The gifts are given to please Him and Him alone. Not all can preach. Not all can prophesy. Not everybody has tongues or the discerning of spirits. This is true of every gift, and we should all be grateful for it. Wouldn't life be boring if we were all trying to operate the same way at the same time while all else is neglected or ignored? It simply wouldn't work and wouldn't constitute a healthy church body. That would be a cult.

The Indivisible Body of Christ

> And the eye cannot say unto the hand, I have no need of thee: nor again the head to the feet, I have no need of you. Nay, much more those members of the body, which seem to be more feeble, are necessary.
>
> —1 CORINTHIANS 12:21–22

In other words, the eye can't look at the hand and say, "Hey, I'm gonna chop you off with a skill saw because you're of no value to me whatsoever." No, each of us is of tremendous value to the body and is indispensable. Don't miss the meaning of that word. It means essential, necessary, and not optional. If you think a local church can properly operate without the entire body operating in the anointing of the Holy Spirit, you'd have to dismiss this passage of the Bible. Even the weakest members operating through the weakest level of their gifting are indispensable.

Accessing our gifts in the context of the body is not an option. I believe the "greater things than these" that Jesus promised will begin to manifest when we start to take God seriously concerning His anointing (John 14:12). We all need to recognize our gifts and let God flow through us, or we're refusing to obey God on this matter. It's that simple. Knowing this, imagine how much more fruitful and powerful a local church would become if every born-again believer operated in the fullness of their gifts—by believing in and accessing the anointing.

Now I beseech you, brethren, by the name of our Lord Jesus Christ, that ye all speak the same thing, and that there be no divisions among you; but that ye be perfectly joined together in the same mind and in the same judgment.

—1 CORINTHIANS 1:10

5

IT'S NOT ABOUT US

*And the King shall answer and say unto them, Verily I
say unto you, Inasmuch as ye have done it unto one of the
least of these my brethren, ye have done it unto me.*
—JESUS (MATTHEW 25:40)

A S WE CONTINUE our expository study of Paul's discourse on the
gifts in 1 Corinthians 12, God begins to zero in on the hurdles
we must cross in the church. Sadly, many church leaders tend to
devalue folks who can't help them achieve their agenda according
to their standards.

They dismiss the value of church members who are less experienced or less admired, and that's a grievous sin of omission. So
much so that Paul wrote we should do the opposite:

> And those members of the body, which we think to be less
> honourable, upon these we bestow more abundant honour;
> and our uncomely parts have more abundant comeliness. For
> our comely parts have no need: but God hath tempered the

69

body together, having given more abundant honour to that part which lacked. That there should be no schism in the body; but that the members should have the same care one for another.

—1 CORINTHIANS 12:23–25

Many pastors handle their church body as if the smaller, less noticeable parts (members) can't make a difference, and this verse proves they're wrong. God wired the body of Christ to thrive best when the gifts of the least are given greater attention.

Every part matters to Him, so every member must matter to us. Every gift holder must be given an avenue to serve Him and minister to the body. They have unrecognized divine potential that we are commanded to nurture and honor, and every church needs to improve in this area, mine included.

God loves to shock us by placing the miraculous in the least likely person—consider David before he was called out by God (1 Sam. 16:11). He was deemed so young and so weak in comparison to his brothers that his father didn't even invite him to Samuel's anointing party. But once "the Spirit of the LORD came upon David" (1 Sam. 16:13), he destroyed Goliath with a slingshot and went on to birth the most important nation on earth.

As our current passage from Paul's discourse teaches (v. 25 above), ignoring the anointing among the least is divisive and in direct opposition to the will of God. He doesn't call us the body of Christ—His literal body—to be cute. If you truly love Him, you'll love, honor, recruit, and seek to activate every part of His body— especially the least.

In the Old Testament, we learn that some victorious kings of antiquity would cut off the thumbs and toes of the opposing king once taken prisoner (Judg. 1:6). When I first learned this years ago, the thumbs made sense, but I used to wonder—why the big toes?

They did this because it would greatly reduce their ability to keep balance.

When you can't keep your balance, you can't stand, and when you can't stand, you can't fight. When the body of Christ is out of balance from lack of obedience to this teaching, we leave ourselves vulnerable to the wiles of the devil, and we can't properly fight back.

Supernatural Interdependence

> And whether one member suffer, all the members suffer with
> it; or one member be honoured, all the members rejoice with
> it. Now ye are the body of Christ, and members in particular.
> —1 CORINTHIANS 12:26–27

Have you ever had a toothache, and as a result, your whole body hurt? The last time I had a toothache, my legs and back hurt, and by the time I got to the dentist, my whole body hurt. A body is a living organism comprised of smaller living organisms that are interconnected and entirely interdependent. The same is true for the body of Christ.

Likewise, if you win a contest and receive a trophy for your victory, doesn't your entire body tingle with joy and excitement? When someone in the body is exalted and used by God, we should never feel envy, jealousy, or bitterness. Instead, we should feel excitement, joy, and gratitude that God saw fit to equip them to do something that brings honor to His body, no matter how minor that victory may seem compared to others.

In the parable of the sower (also called the parable of the three soils), Jesus said that some of us would produce thirty-fold, some fifty-fold, and some one-hundred-fold through our ministry. So, all who are born again will produce measurable fruit (Matt. 13:1–23), and it's on us if that's not true of the least in our local churches.

God Alone Appoints

And God hath set some in the church, first apostles, second-
arily prophets, thirdly teachers, after that miracles, then gifts
of healings, helps, governments, diversities of tongues.

—1 CORINTHIANS 12:28

In verse 28 of Paul's discourse, we see that "God hath set some
(appointed) in the church." God appoints, not your preacher, church
leaders, denominational hierarchy, seminary, granddaddy, or tradi-
tion. Just God. Notice that this verse also points out that the gifts
are given within the context of the New Testament church that
was born at the first Pentecost (Acts 2), as discussed in this book's
introduction.

Because of the error of cessationism, some argue that Paul was
writing in the context of the Old Testament, but that's not the
case. Paul wrote that—upon establishing His church—God first
appointed apostles, then prophets, then teachers. Don't confuse
these gifts with the titles of the same name.

The special title of apostle was reserved for the handful of first-
century heroes who were eyewitnesses and ear-witnesses to the
resurrected Jesus (1 Cor. 9:1) and were personally called into this
anointing by Jesus (Gal. 1:1). Though the apostolic gift continues
today to equip the church with leaders of leaders, I'm not convinced
that anyone has reason to carry the title today.

I know some folks with this gift do, in fact, carry the title and
view it as an official office in their hierarchy, and I won't judge their
motives. I'm just not a big title guy, and I honestly don't believe
there is a real need for someone to carry that title, even if they
indeed have that anointing.

The Five-Fold Ministry Gifts

Considering the three major categories noted in the introduction (manifestation, ministry, and motivation) in the context of verse 28 above, we can see that the gifts of apostles, prophets, and teachers are in the category of ministry gifts. Keep in mind that the gifts can be in multiple categories (teaching is a prime example), so don't let that confuse you as we proceed.

Though Paul names just three of the ministry gifts here, he identifies five such gifts in Ephesians 4:11–13—apostles, prophets, evangelists, pastors, and teachers. In the modern church, this category of gifts is commonly called the five-fold ministry. Because the ministry gifts deal more with the role of these gifts within church government and the leadership structure of the various types of church communities, I'll be reserving their deeper study for a future text.

This small book is just the beginning of this journey into the supernatural workings of God, so I'll focus on the two categories that are far more pressing for most of us—the gifts of manifestation and the gifts of motivation. To help you keep it all sorted out, up until verse 28 of this discourse, Paul has only mentioned gifts from the perspective of the manifestation category.

When I first read this verse while preparing for this book, I thought, "How could I have missed that before?" I knew about major prophets and the minor prophets of the Old Testament, and I was convinced by my seminary that they were no longer needed after the first century. As we know now, we were mistaken. God clearly puts people with a prophetic anointing in the church for the sake of the body. I'm a witness.

That said, prophecy is a gift that requires a lot of maturity. A legitimate prophecy from God will never bring undue attention or credence to the person speaking or writing the prophecy, and that can be difficult for those who are immature or new to the faith. As we now know, every gift must edify other individuals in the body to the glory of God, not the gift holder. The same is true for those with the gift of teaching and the other ministry gifts, as well as the offices that appropriate their names into their titles.

Many Gifts, One Body

As Paul begins to close his discourse on the gifts, he names several wide-ranging gifts that aren't intended to serve as a comprehensive list. Instead, he mentions several such gifts to ensure we know that every type of gift is subject to the same basic caveats. While he's clearly emphasizing the first three that he numbered, in verse 28 he also mentions "miracles, then gifts of healing, helps, governments, [and] diversities of tongues," not to set them higher than the others but to underscore this all-inclusive approach to addressing the gifts.

In fact, with closer inspection, you can see that some of these gifts represent categories of gifts. For example, "diversities of tongues," as discussed earlier, represent variations of the same gift, and "gifts of healing" cover a broad variety of infirmities and wounds. So if you're struggling to figure out your gifts, you can imagine how many specific abilities fall under "helps" and "governments."

Some pastors have the gift of administration (governments), but they don't have the gift of teaching. Someone who leads a church of five thousand people might put the flock to sleep five minutes into their sermon, but because they are anointed administrators gifted at delegating and empowering others, their church still grows in the Spirit.

Some pastors are great at shepherding their people but are weak communicators, and some pastors are great communicators but not nearly as effective as pastors. When they are operating in the Spirit, God honors them regardless, and He actively does that through the anointing that rests upon the full church body.

> And he said unto me, My grace is sufficient for thee: for my
> strength is made perfect in weakness. Most gladly therefore
> will I rather glory in my infirmities, that the power of Christ
> may rest upon me.
>
> —2 CORINTHIANS 12:9

As I continue this journey, I am trying to figure out God's proper balance between my preaching and pastoring. I aim to be a good preacher and a good shepherd. Ultimately, what difference will I make if I can communicate well with the microphone but can't help you through your brokenness?

I know I am surrounded by gifted folks who can partner with me in these roles, so I'm confident that the needs of our church will be met in this regard. I also firmly believe I'm called to operate at a high level through both gifts. As I recognize my weaknesses, I trust the power of Christ will grow in me while empowering others in our church to stand in the gaps where I am weak.

Administrations and Governments

In verse 28 of Paul's discourse, he also speaks to the gift of governments (or administrations). At Global Vision Bible Church, this is represented by our unconditional love for people, expressed through our extravagant generosity and radical mercy. Mercy can be considered a manifestation of the gift of helps, and our church was born from my call to extend mercy in unprecedented ways.

Some people have a high-end gift of mercy, so they work well in food ministries and clothing distribution. An outreach pastor can exhibit an amazing ability to lift up homeless folks, drug addicts, and people that are beaten down and hurting. Why? Because they have a spiritual gift of helps. As you ponder these gifts, I'm sure you can identify many areas of need where someone with this gift could change many lives.

In the KJV, the word *administrations* in other translations is translated as "governments." This points to the fact that some people in the church are gifted to get involved in the administration of government and other world systems where the gospel is needed. Though we focus first on the body of Christ, never forget that we are commissioned by Jesus to "Go into all the world and proclaim the gospel to the whole creation" (Mark 16:15, ESV).

For this, we know that some people have this governmental, administrative, authoritative gifting that makes them especially influential within the legal and organizational structures of entities outside the church. People with this gift can make strong Spirit-filled politicians—if there can be such a thing. I believe there should be.

These folks are empowered to touch people in ways others cannot because they have an anointed pizzazz about them. Imagine how beautiful the nations would be if born-again believers with this gift took over the world's governments. I believe the Lord has gifted many of you for that purpose, for the sake of the gospel.

Speaking of Tongues

Notice that Paul again mentions "diversities of tongues" in his closing statements. This is especially interesting because he made sure he mentions tongues in the context of the church—even though it's not a gift that everyone will have. Of course, this is true of every gift. I emphasize this here to ensure you ignore people who say, "According to the Bible, you're not filled with the Holy Spirit until you've spoken in tongues." Don't listen to that lawless nonsense.

In the Bible, the only church mentioned outside the Book of Acts that ever spoke in tongues was the church at Corinth, and they were way out of order in the way they were doing it. This is why Paul emphasized it in his first letter to them, and from what I've seen, that's still a problem today. Ultimately, I want whatever God wants for me. I'll take every drop of it unashamedly and unapologetically. But do not let people bully you and beat you into submission, making you think you need a particular gift that God might never have given you. As we've discussed, God plainly states that He doesn't give each gift to every person. Knowing that should help free many people from super-spiritual legalists. Don't listen to them.

You Be You

> Are all apostles? are all prophets? are all teachers? are all workers of miracles? Have all the gifts of healing? do all speak with tongues? do all interpret?
>
> —1 CORINTHIANS 12:29–30

As we close Paul's discourse on the gifts from 1 Corinthians 12, we see him hammer home a crucial point. No one has all the gifts. He asks, "Are all apostles?" Obviously not. "Are all prophets?" Thank God, no. Most of the time, prophets are pretty demonstrative. They're usually very bold and in your face. We can't all be like that, nor should we all want to be like that. We've got to have some nice, calm, sweet-spirited folks in the church too!

"Are all teachers?" Obviously not. I can't toss every one of you a microphone to preach all willy-nilly, nor would I. Not everybody has the gift to teach. We face this major problem within the church today—and it's a big reason God led me to write this book—we put people in areas they're not gifted for. As a result of this misplacement, folks get burned out and often burned up. It won't end well if you're trying to operate in an area you're not gifted for.

"Are all workers of miracles?" No. God has mysterious reasons for how He distributes the gifts, but we can be sure He is aware that some people don't have the capacity or the humility to handle certain gifts, while others do. "Do all speak with tongues?" Nope. "Do all interpret?" Certainly not.

A local church does best when we are all operating in the

gifts that God gave us and nothing more. For me, less is more, so I love delegating things I cannot do. I've learned that this approach serves me well as I encourage the flock to operate in their anointing.

The More Excellent Way

> But covet earnestly the best gifts: and yet shew I unto you a more excellent way.
> —1 CORINTHIANS 12:31

After that string of humbling reminders, Paul tells you and me to "earnestly covet the best gifts." He's telling you to pray for all God has for you, especially if you have a genuine affinity for a particular gift. This is a supernaturally exciting instruction, as it tells us to lift our heads and expectantly look to Him for gifts of the highest need in the body. These may be gifts we have yet to discover, and they may be gifts that we know we have but hope to see manifest at a higher level.

To earnestly covet is to desire something you don't just passively wait for. Paul is telling us to seek the gifts through intense study of the Word and intentional prayer. All the gifts are readily available in the church for the purposes God revealed in this discourse, but— as is true of the born-again life in general—we must embrace His process to access them in their fullness.

I absolutely love how Paul closes this discourse by telling us that God will show us "a more excellent way." Wait, "What?" He just went through a whole chapter emphasizing the power and beauty in the gifts. Why does he now say there's a more excellent way? I find it incredibly beautiful that God chose to pivot in this way, and you'll soon see what I mean. It's a wonderful example of God's character and divine order in all He does through us.

As we turn the chapter (both in this book and in the Bible), it might have occurred to you that this entire discourse on spiritual gifts would be obsolete if they had ever ceased. That's a lot of Bible with much more to come, so thank God the gifts of the Holy Spirit are alive and well.

> If a son shall ask bread of any of you that is a father, will he give him a stone? or if he ask a fish, will he for a fish give him a serpent? Or if he shall ask an egg, will he offer him a scorpion? If ye then, being evil, know how to give good gifts unto your children: how much more shall your heavenly Father give the Holy Spirit to them that ask him?
>
> —Jesus (Luke 11:11–13)

6

What's Love Got to Do With It?

Beloved, let us love one another: for love is of God; and every one that loveth is born of God, and knoweth God. He that loveth not knoweth not God; for God is love. In this was manifested the love of God toward us, because that God sent his only begotten Son into the world, that we might live through him.
—1 John 4:7–9

As discussed earlier, even those who are not yet believers have been given good gifts with attributes similar to spiritual gifts, but only those of us who are born of God (born again) have the Holy Spirit indwelling us to supernaturally empower these gifts. Likewise, even among the born again, it's one thing to utilize the gifts in service to the local church and its members and an entirely different thing to make sure it is done in the right spirit.

Never forget being born again is both an event *and* a process. To quote John the Baptist, it is the baptism of "the Holy Ghost and with fire" (Luke 3:16). The apostle John encapsulated this truth in the passage above. It's wonderful for us to preach, pray, give, and see healings through the anointing, but every bit of that is futile if it doesn't come from a place of love, for "God is love."

Historically and theologically, 1 Corinthians 13 is often referred to as the love chapter, and rightly so. It comprises one of the most famous discourses in the history of literature, and it expands on John's "God is love" axiom in one of the most life-applicable passages in all the Bible. In the love chapter, Paul details how God's love is the vehicle through which the gifts are properly used and enhanced.

On the heels of teaching us how to understand, access, and utilize our spiritual gifts, God ensures we know that there are specific *ways* in which the gifts must flow through us to others.

These ways flow from the very heart of God, and it can be said that this flow manifests the very life of Christ within us.

When I'm preaching, I want people to say I enhanced their life somehow. I want to know that I encouraged them, edified them, and gave them something they did not already have. I never want to wrap up my preaching and have somebody wipe their brow and say, "I'm glad that cat's done." I would rather preach shorter sermons, leaving people in the presence of God and hungry for more, than preach longer sermons and bore people to tears. That can only be done if I preach through love.

What Is This Love?

> Though I speak with the tongues of men and of angels, and have not charity, I am become as sounding brass, or a tinkling cymbal.
>
> —1 CORINTHIANS 13:1

While the word *charity* has a well-known common meaning, in the King James English it speaks to unconditional, selfless, godly love. Over time, the word *charity* became synonymous with Christian love, which is the origin of modern charity. That preaches, amen? It means that I am to love you the way Jesus loves me, and that can only be done by administering the Holy Spirit anointing in me, poured out for your benefit. That's true charity.

People often cite spiritual gifts without considering the crucial caveat Paul calls the "more excellent way" (1 Corinthians 12:31, as cited at the end of our previous chapter). If you read 1 Corinthians in full, you'll notice that Paul's love chapter (13) is a seamless continuation of his spiritual gifts discourse, so the gifts should never be discussed apart from a focus on love. No matter my gifts, I must access them through godly love—charity. It's the highest form of love we can share with others, so keep that in mind as we proceed.

By saying there is a much better way to utilize the gifts, God is telling us that His love in us is far more powerful than the workings of the spiritual gifts in and of themselves. Many readers will just brush over this while studying the gifts as if love is an afterthought or a closing garnish to the Lord, and we need to correct that in the church.

Whether you can speak well or jump high, if love is not the starting point or foundation, it will never accomplish its divine purpose. It will not only be useless, but it will also be an irritant to God. For this, the more excellent way is not simply knowing your gifts and learning how to use them. It's learning to operate in them through the expression of the love of Christ.

Christian Love?

Have you ever heard a high school band that wasn't playing in tune? It's the most fall-down-the-steps, ear-damage-inducing nightmare you'll ever hear. Regardless of the band's size, it's excruciating when they're not playing from the same sheet of music. Through verse 1 of the love chapter, God is telling us—the church—that we need to get on the same page in the hymnal. If we're not doing it through love, it's just a bunch of disharmony, dysfunction, and disunity.

> We know that we have passed from death unto life, because we love the brethren. He that loveth not his brother abideth in death.
>
> —1 John 3:14

Let me go further within the context of godly love and exhort you with a challenging truth. Don't let anyone guilt you into thinking that you are called to love lost people like you are called to love God's people in the church (born-again believers, the brethren, the remnant, the elect). We are called to love everyone with a generalized type of love, but when the Bible says that we are to love the brethren or a brother, He's not talking about the lost. He's talking about the body of Christ.

I am not called to lay down my life for the world. Jesus already did that. I'm called to lay down my life for "the brethren" (1 John 3:16; see also John 15:13). There is a huge difference. Problems arise when we try to love saved people while acting like lost people—absent of *His* love. We are commanded to love the brethren in unity and harmony, and we should never try to partner with the lost in the same way. We're to love all people enough to preach the gospel to them and work tirelessly to lead them out of darkness, but we can never love them the way we are commanded to love our brothers and sisters in Christ.

As the Word of God constantly reminds us, "We know that we are from God, and the whole world lies in the power of the evil one" (1 John 5:19, ESV). The apostle Paul stated this with great detail when he wrote, "Be ye not unequally yoked together with unbelievers: for what fellowship hath righteousness with unrighteousness? and what communion hath light with darkness?" (2 Cor. 6:14). Love them like neighbors, but not like family in the body of

Christ—until they truly are. We could rattle off many reasons for this much-ignored command of God, but His Word should suffice.

Conversely, I want to caution you about a common pitfall. Some people will selfishly try to use their gift to gain influence or power in the ministry, opening doors or more opportunities for themselves. If God wants to open doors and give you opportunities, that's a blessing worth celebrating. I will rejoice with those who rejoice and weep with those who weep (Rom. 12:15), but this cannot come through selfish motives (Phil. 2:3–4), as that would be demonic. We must never access the gifts for ourselves. We operate in the anointing to the glory of God, not the glory of us, so I must use my gifts for your edification, not my own. Please don't forget that.

When Love Offends

> And though I have the gift of prophecy, and understand all mysteries, and all knowledge; and though I have all faith, so that I could remove mountains, and have not charity, I am nothing.
>
> —1 CORINTHIANS 13:2

When I preach, I take great care to do it in love, so don't be mistaken when I'm bold and dogmatic. Contrary to popular accusations, I never preach from a place of hate. Though I hate the devil and the evil he sows, I love the people under his control. I call out their sinful ways to expose the enemy's work in their lives, and that is, without question, an act of love. In the same way, you can be sure I hate a lot about this world's wicked organizations and cultural perversions, but that doesn't mean I don't love the people who operate through them.

Love is never expressed through approval or tolerance of sin—on the contrary. If I truly love someone headed for hell, I will say and do all I can to wake them up before it's too late, even if I offend them to the point that they call me hateful. In the same way, if I ever witness someone trying to break into your house to murder you or run away with your children, you'd better know I'm going to do all I can to stop them. That also is an act of love.

In verse 2 of the love chapter, Paul restates the love caveat being true for even the most powerful of gifts. The gifts are worthless to God unless they are expressed in operation through, and are motivated by, His love. Paul speaks to this when he says that without love, "I am nothing." Have you ever met someone full of faith and mean-spirited at the same time? Those two things don't go together, as one counteracts the other. If Paul, the man who wrote fourteen books of the Bible, can say he is nothing without love, you'd better know it's also true of you and me.

It Will Profit You Nothing

And though I bestow all my goods to feed the poor, and though I give my body to be burned, and have not charity, it profiteth me nothing.

—1 CORINTHIANS 13:3

In verse 3, Paul reinforces that the love requirement applies to the gifts no matter how self-sacrificing you may be. I can give up all I have to help the poor, but if godly love wasn't my motivating force, if it wasn't done for God's glory *and* the benefit of others, it's worth nothing. Just before He laid down His life on the cross to save us all, Jesus taught that self-sacrifice is indeed expected but that loving mercy is far more important (Matt. 9:13).

Beware thinking that sacrifice alone impresses God. That's works-based religion, and there is no love in that nonsense. Even if I die a martyr, what good is it if I don't do it in love? If I don't act through sheer godly love, "it profiteth me nothing"—absolutely nothing!

If your desire for honor, admiration, or personal gain plays a role in your sacrifices, don't think for one minute that Jesus will say "well done" when you see Him face to face. We can lie to ourselves about our motives, but we can't fool Him, and He will never reward us for this form of dishonesty, no matter how great our sacrifice.

In the Book of Acts, we learn that Ananias and his wife Sapphira did exactly that, and God was so infuriated that He struck them dead for all to see (Acts 5:3–5). When God names people in the Bible for their sins, you don't ever want to risk making their mistakes. Be very careful what you lay at the feet of God.

Extravagant giving is one of my highest gifts, so you'd better believe I take great care to check my heart before I stroke a check. I celebrate God's generosity and the people He blesses through our church, but I never consider how it personally blesses me. In fact, I know I will come under severe persecution for being so generous, but I'm neither motivated nor deterred by what people think about me or my motives. God knows I act only through love, and His approval is all that matters to me.

How Love Is Produced

Charity suffereth long, and is kind; charity envieth not; charity vaunteth not itself, is not puffed up.

—1 CORINTHIANS 13:4

We mostly hear these next few verses of the love chapter in a marriage ceremony, as if they're strictly speaking to a husband and wife. But God is teaching us how to treat each other in the local church. This is how I'm supposed to treat you, how you're supposed to treat me, and how we are both to treat all others around us. This is the way that God produces more love in us over time, for "charity suffereth long."

In our churches, we tend to give up too quickly on people who don't perform the way we think they should. We say things like,

"Well, that knucklehead is never gonna get off those pills," or, "That chick is never gonna get off meth," or, "That family is never gonna quit doing this or doing that." Love, the Bible says, suffereth long! We need to put up with the frustrations and long sleepless nights so that we can love people to Christ. Yes, the Lord may eventually prune them out if they remain unrepentant, but that's His decision according to His timing, not ours.

None of us just pulled ourselves into the born-again life by our own bootstraps. We're all the products of someone's relentless love, intense prayer life, or long-suffering discipleship.

The Golden Rule

Verse 4 also says that love is kind, but kindness has become a lost art. Many think of kindness as a weakness, but the opposite is true. Anybody can be a jerk, and that's weak. Anyone can be mean-spirited, but the Bible says that a godly person is kind even to the animals, let alone the people we're trying to rescue (Prov. 12:10).

I don't even like dogs or cats—aside from our puppy Whitfield because he's just super cool and precious, praise God—but you can be sure I'm kind to all of them nonetheless. If I can be kind to an animal, don't you think I can be kind to a human I'm commanded to love? Don't you think you should be kind to that server, that mechanic changing your tire, or that lady in Walmart who's frustrating you? Sometimes we think we're these amazing Christians when the truth is we're not even *kind*, and that's ungodly. We must handle people with care and kindness because people are fragile, and all are precious to God.

Have you ever noticed how breakable we are and how easily we get our feelings hurt? Do you know why that is? It's because people *need* kindness. So if you think you can righteously use your gifts while being mean or dismissive, you're wrong.

Sometimes folks tell me, "Pastor Locke, people just aren't kind to me," and I tell them, "It's probably because you're not being kind *to them*." This points to what we call the Golden Rule, as Jesus said:

> Therefore all things whatsoever ye would that men should do to you, do ye even so to them: for this is the law and the prophets.
>
> —MATTHEW 7:12

Jesus also said, "Give, and it shall be given unto you; good measure, pressed down, and shaken together, and running over" (Luke 6:38). He's not talking about money here, but about forgiveness and love—He's talking about acceptance and mercy. "A man that hath friends must shew himself friendly" (Prov. 18:24). If no one smiles at you at church, it's because you walk around looking like a grouch.

If you smile, you'll get a smile; if you hug, you'll get a hug. In counseling sessions, guys often say, "Pastor, my wife just does not understand me." So, I ask them how much effort and time they put into trying to understand her. If you want understanding, you must give understanding. Give, and it shall be given to you.

Check Your Pride

Returning to verse 4 of the love chapter, we see, "charity envieth not." This is an especially important direction for the local church, where folks can easily become jealous of what other people have. Some people can't even rejoice for someone else's new vehicle because theirs is an old jalopy, and God hasn't yet answered their prayers to replace it.

We often think, "Oh my goodness, how dare God in heaven bless them over me when I've been praying about this need for so long!" God has never made a mistake, and He doesn't need your permission to bless somebody else.

We ought to rejoice with folks when they get a new house. We ought to rejoice when the church down the street has a bigger

Sunday service than we have. We ought to rejoice when somebody receives a blessing from God. The Bible says real charity "envieth not." I want you to be blessed! I don't have jealousy in my heart; I want to see others excel, and it blesses me when they are blessed. That's what love does.

Verse 4 also says, "charity vaunteth not its own." That means don't jump out in front of others to be seen in the brighter light. Many people try to operate in their gifts by jockeying for position or attention, and there's no Christlike love in that, but only self-love. In the full context of verse 4, Paul also tells us that the selfless love we are called to is "not puffed up." You would think this means the same thing as "vaunteth not," but they actually speak to two different forms of selfishness.

To be puffed up is to walk around with your chest all bowed out like a cocky banty rooster. They walk around with an air that says, "Oh, look at me. I'm so blessed of the Lord." If you have to tell me you're filled with the Holy Ghost, you're not! If you have to brag about how spiritual you are, you aren't.

Some people just love to puff themselves up, and it seems they're the only ones who can't see that their pride keeps getting bigger and bigger, and that's *never* real godly love. It certainly isn't selfless or Christlike. Godly love—charity—wants to make Jesus the focus of everyone and everything by elevating others, never ourselves. If you want to be like Jesus, you'll trust Him to position you as you walk, speak, and live in sincere humility. That's the attitude that expresses real love.

For whosoever exalteth himself shall be abased; and he that humbleth himself shall be exalted.

—Jesus (Luke 14:11)

Behavior Is Fruit

From there, Paul shifts from calling out the sin of pride to calling out acts of evil. In verse 5, still speaking of love, he writes:

Doth not behave itself unseemly, seeketh not her own, is not easily provoked, thinketh no evil.

—1 Corinthians 13:5

The word *unseemly* means inappropriate, which in the context of the Bible, is unrighteous. He's saying that real love does not compromise the truth through a charade of deceptive false pretense. Real love—true charity—does not behave in unseemly ways, and it never operates through unrighteous motivations.

If you hear someone say, "If you love me, you will [fill in the blank]," you need to rebuke that wicked manipulation. That is not love; it's a learned behavior that breeds bondage and can ruin people's lives for a very long time. This is why denominational religion keeps people at arm's length. They love people with false expectations and religious conditions, which is *unseemly*. They often pretend to love you as long as you give, serve, or do as they say.

Real love will never do this. It's pure, and it "seeketh not her own." In our weekly men's Bible study at Global Vision, I frequently point out that love, wisdom, and grace are always expressed with feminine terms in the Bible. Have you ever noticed that? They're always personified as a woman, and not once in the Bible are they personified as a man. God tells us that real love is marked with a brand of tenderness that cannot be dismissed. This is what He means by saying that love doesn't seek "her" own way.

Let's go back to the sin of pride. To fully understand this phrase, it's important to know that pride is the source of all contention (Prov. 13:10). When two people can't get along, when factions divide within a local church, and when a nation can't work toward a united purpose, it's always a matter of sinful pride, as there's a lack of tenderness and empathy by one or more parties.

When someone comes to me and says, "We both love the Lord, but we just can't get along," I know that someone is lying. Someone loves *self* more than Jesus; far more than they love the other person. My Bible says that real love does not seek her own, so stop arguing from a place of pride and contention. Real love is deferential to others, not *self*.

No Offense

Verse 5 then says that love is "not easily provoked." I've found that most people blame their anger and contention issues on their upbringing, but we must stop blaming our parents when we act like a jerk. In counseling sessions, people often say, "Well, you know, I just have this habit of blowing up every now and again." Yes, and a shotgun only has to go off once to kill someone. The words you say in a fit of anger can ruin someone else for a very long time, as there is no love in it. If you think you can effectively access your anointing before you deal with your pride and anger, wrong again, bucko.

> Great peace have they which love thy law: and nothing shall offend them.
> —Psalm 119:165

The Bible says nothing can offend someone who truly loves the Word of God. So, if *anything* can offend you, you'd better memorize that verse and learn to love it. Don't just read over this with complacency or an "I can't do that" mentality. If you love Jesus, you're going to love the Bible. You will read it, obey it, memorize it, and love it, and it will, in turn, bring you great peace.

When we are in a situation or season where we must endure sustained evil, we might eventually reach a state of righteous anger. (See Jesus flipping tables in the temple in Matthew 21:12.) But we must never become offended. Take a moment to truly consider the difference. In contrast to righteous anger, which can be entirely selfless, offense—like its partner contention—is always rooted in selfish pride. As you might have noticed, offense is an especially dark spirit in these last days. Sadly, the reasons church folks get offended are the same reasons lost folks get offended, and both are equally ignorant of the Word of God on this matter.

All About Communication

The phrase "not easily provoked" is especially beautiful in the context of marriage. A spiritually healthy marriage will never be characterized by constant fighting. There's no real love in that.

Born-again believers will not be easily provoked to displays of anger or passive aggression in marriage. So, if you and your spouse commonly hold grudges and walk around ignoring each other, you'd better repent of that nonsense, or you'll never be able to access your anointing as designed.

The number one problem in America (and in the church) is poor communication, and that's the reason people are so easily provoked. In counseling sessions, folks come to me with all sorts of problems, and I've discovered that most of their problems are never the real problem. The root is almost always the lack of communication.

Having said that, note that the Bible doesn't say love can never be provoked to anger because it definitely can when it's righteous (biblical). But when your anger is righteous and justified, it will never linger. The Bible tells us that righteous anger will not remain in us past the setting of the sun (Eph. 4:26), which points to our need to communicate honestly and work through the problem.

Allowing anger to manifest in a way that burdens you through the night is sinful to God. This is why we need to be bold in our communications when driven to anger. Too many folks are afraid to deal with the problems that cause their anger, but they need to get over themselves and just do what's right in God's sight—address it with the ones who provoke the anger. This is why I originally posted video rants against evil and perversion in this nation. If I hadn't gotten it off my chest, I never would have been able to sleep. I trust you get my point.

If you're one of those people who boast about your short temper, you'd better know that's unrighteous nonsense. If that's you, your short fuse is not the other person's fault; it's your fault. Do not be easily provoked, says the Lord. The Lord blesses us with the ability to submit to the Holy Spirit, and a quick temper is never righteous (Prov. 15:18).

If you think I just fly off the handle all willy-nilly when I call out evil in my preaching or my videos, you're mistaken. I am very prayerful and patient in my efforts to bring change and calculated in what I say when I finally have to call something out in a public forum. But when it starts to rob my peace and my sleep, I know the Holy Spirit is moving me to speak out. When provoked, though we need to resist anger as long as possible, we also need to obey the Holy Spirit's leading—especially when your gifting involves matters of wisdom, knowledge, and prophecy (John 16:13)—as that's an outworking of real love.

Counterfeit Discernment

At the end of verse 5, we see that real love "thinketh no evil." If we're honest, even the most mature among us will admit this is a very difficult command because we're all wired to think evil of people in this fallen world. It's human nature, but it's not the Holy Spirit's nature, so we all need to refine that out of our thinking processes.

This sort of thinking feeds our fleshly desire to feel better about ourselves or to justify our unrighteous fears. Some who think they have the spirit of discernment are operating in its wicked counterfeit—the spirit of suspicion.

When the adulterous woman was brought to Jesus by the Pharisees, the Bible says He ignored them while writing in the dirt (John 8:6). The next time someone comes to you with a bunch of gossip-filled suspicions, just fall on your knees and start doodling on the ground. They'll probably leave you alone and never come back! Seriously, don't be quick to believe evil the first time you hear it. Knowing the truth from the beginning is far less important than ensuring love guides your thought processes and helps you avoid false assumptions. We must allow love to guide us as we work toward restoration and reconciliation to the truth (Gal. 6:1).

> Speak not evil one of another, brethren. He that speaketh evil of his brother, and judgeth his brother, speaketh evil of the law, and judgeth the law: but if thou judge the law, thou art not a doer of the law, but a judge.
>
> —JAMES 4:11

7

The Complexity and Greatness of Love

Rejoiceth not in iniquity, but rejoiceth in the truth.
—1 CORINTHIANS 13:6

As WE CONTINUE our expository study of the love chapter, in verse 6, we learn that real love doesn't rejoice in something you know is evil (iniquity) according to God. This is why—even in efforts of compassion and kindness—we cannot participate in or approve of LGBTQ sin. How can I rejoice in that perversion? I cannot.

The Bible alone can define and explain real love and the commands of God, and we are commanded to celebrate His love and His truth alone. This is a very polarizing subject in this relativistic, godless culture, but we cannot shy away from it. I know that I can be so bold and demonstrative about this subject that it upsets folks, but as noted earlier, this is an act of obedience to God and, therefore, an act of real love.

> What I tell you in darkness, that speak ye in light: and what ye
> hear in the ear, that preach ye upon the housetops.
> —JESUS (MATTHEW 10:27)

As a pastor and teacher of the Word operating in the gifts God has given me, I am compelled to boldly preach and teach the truth as led by the Holy Spirit, no matter how abrasive it may seem. At the same time, I do all I can to love people no matter where they are in life, not just when they're where I want them to be.

God's grace alone can change people, so I love the deceived and wounded. I truly do. At Global Vision Bible Church, we accept everyone just as they are but never approve of the sin that keeps them in iniquity. How can we rejoice in acts God calls unseemly and immoral (1 Cor. 6:9)? We cannot.

There's a big difference between acceptance and approval. I honestly don't fret over your lifestyle choices, but that doesn't mean I can ignore the Bible and approve of them. I will continue to preach the Word of God no matter who it offends, and when the Holy Spirit compels me to stick my neck out to expose evil in the public forum, I simply obey.

We must operate in our gifts as He leads, not as people desire, and I certainly can't bow to the culture when it says we have to ignore the Bible when it offends the lost. That's not real love. We're on a mission to rescue lost folks from the horrors of hell, and there's no easy way to do that. We simply cannot compromise the truth of Scripture, no matter who it angers or what they say about us.

As noted earlier, compromise is why the world and the church are in such dire straits today, and the Bible warned that this would happen. Pride is an abomination to God (Prov. 16:5), so pride in iniquity must be a double abomination. If you don't know this by now, I need you to realize that not everything folks characterize as love is love, so don't let your compassion blind you to the counterfeit. Iniquity can never partner with real love. Sometimes that which people call love is simply rebellion against God and the Bible, and contrary to popular opinion, sometimes it's simply lust and perversion.

Time-Out: It's All About the Children

We have raised an entire generation of people who say we need to stay out of people's bedrooms, yet they won't even stay out of our public schools, Disney and Nickelodeon, or even a Kellogg's cereal box. Their perversion is pushed on our children wherever they look in this demon-possessed culture. Unfortunately, we knew a long time ago that the legalization of perversion—starting with same-sex marriage in 2015—was just the beginning of their destructive slippery slope to destruction.

They said all they wanted was for gay folks to be able to marry in private, and if we would just give them that, they promised to let it end there. I need you to realize right now that it was never about gay marriage. It has always been about perverting children and indoctrinating them into pedophilia and other evil perversions. Same-sex marriage was just their Trojan horse, and pedophiles in high places have been driving this plan for a very long time.

It may shock you that I put that in print, but a true pastor will always tell you the truth, no matter how bad it hurts. Real love doesn't compromise the truth or remain silent when children are in such horrifying danger. So if you're celebrating or condoning iniquity, please stop.

Bear, Believe, Hope, Endure

Beareth all things, believeth all things, hopeth all things, endureth all things.

—1 CORINTHIANS 13:7

In verse 5, we learned that God doesn't want us to think evil of people, and now He's saying He wants us to believe the best about people. As a pastor, I want to live my life in such a way that when someone comes to you spouting nonsensical lies, you readily know that it's not true. If I'm living right, slanderous lies ought to be so out of character that it's hard for you to believe them.

The Bible says, "When a man's ways please the LORD, he maketh even his enemies to be at peace with him" (Prov. 16:7). I was recently reminded of how that works. I was at Dunkin' Donuts early one morning, and a lady who works there has a lifestyle that I'm known to call out from the platform, yet somehow, she still has a genuine affinity for me and our church.

She is super kind every time I go in there, and she always greets me with good cheer, saying, "Hey, Preacher!" She knows exactly how I like my coffee and if I want one cup or two just by the look in my eyes when I walk in.

One day she came and approached me with tears in her eyes and said, "I just want you to know that I saw what CNN did to you. I know those people on that side very well, and I just want you to know that I don't believe a thing they said about you or your church." Then she said, "I don't care what CNN says, you just keep standing up and do what God Almighty has put on your heart because though you're just a customer at Dunkin' Donuts, I know who you really are, and I don't need CNN to tell me that."

You can imagine how she blessed my heart that morning. This is a lady that I see *every* single day at a Dunkin' Donuts, and though she lives a life I can't and won't condone, the consistency of my kindness and love toward her revealed who I really am, and her tears reminded me why I love people no matter their iniquity, no matter what they're going through. That's an example of the fruit produced by real love, and I'll forever love her for who she is to God, not for what she does. And still, none of that silences the truth I must speak.

Do you know what happens when you take hope away from people? They start busting out windows and burning down cities— while burning down their lives along the way. As a pastor, I will always be among the first to call out iniquity, but we must never lose hope for the souls who perpetrate these sins.

They are still precious to God, and we must be willing to bear through the tough times with real love in our hearts if we ever hope to rescue them from their darkness. God gives us the gifts for this very purpose; let's not squander them on ourselves. As verse 7 hammers home, we must never forget that real love "endureth all things." That includes the good, the bad, the up, the down, the right, and even the wrong—the whole deal.

God didn't say this road would be easy, amen? Real love endures *all* as we journey this difficult road in His refining fire, and—as we'll discuss when you turn the page—real love *never* fails, no matter what.

> But I say unto you which hear, Love your enemies, do good to them which hate you, Bless them that curse you, and pray for them which despitefully use you.
>
> —Jesus (Luke 6:27–28)

Even in Part, God Never Fails

> Charity never faileth: but whether there be prophecies, they shall fail; whether there be tongues, they shall cease; whether there be knowledge, it shall vanish away. For we know in

> part, and we prophesy in part. But when that which is perfect
> is come, then that which is in part shall be done away.
>
> —1 Corinthians 13:8–10

We now arrive at the passage in the love chapter that the cessationist doctrine so badly twists. Since we fully explored this passage to correct that lawless doctrine in the Introduction, I'll move on to reinforce the correct contextual points, starting with its thesis in verse 8, "Charity never faileth." Through this verse, Paul reminds us that God is teaching us about His love, agape love, as it applies to His gifts.

When God says love never fails, the emphasis is on the word *never*. His love simply never fails. God in us NEVER fails.

When we properly operate in our spiritual gifts—through God's love—the product and purpose will never fail. Just as the Word of God will never return void, when you use your gifts through this brand of love, you will always produce fruit in your life and the lives of others around you (Isa. 55:9–11). Hate fails, division fails, racism fails, deception fails, tyranny fails, and fear fails, but real love never fails.

With this passage, Paul refocuses on the spiritual gifts to remind us that they are expressly designed for use in this life, on this side of heaven, before they are no longer needed in their partial form. God is telling us to put them to use now, through His love, for the sake of the lost—"before the great and terrible day of the Lord come" (Joel 2:31). The days are indeed growing short, so we need to access the gifts to do good works in the light while it is still day (John 9:4).

Notice in the passage where Paul writes, "for we know in part, and we prophesy in part" (v. 9). While we have the whole Word of God, we also have folks in the body of Christ with these gifts "in part" to encourage us upward by offering personal details that will always stand on the Word. Paul is telling us that—until we're glorified in heaven—these details and the Bible on which they stand will only reveal a portion of the larger prophetic picture. Paul isn't saying the Bible is incomplete, but rather that we'll have to get to heaven before we can understand the full picture.

Not even the most anointed Bible teachers on earth can preach the prophetic timeline in full, so if anyone ever tries to tell you they have a word or a prophecy that either contradicts the Bible or somehow dictates every detail in a matter, you need to rebuke that nonsense and get away from that false prophet. Until we're glorified in heaven—until "that which is perfect" comes (v. 10)—all these gifts offer but a glimpse of the greater glory yet to come. Until then, we will have prophecies, tongues, visions, signs, and wonders that reveal unknowns in part.

Time to Grow Up

When I was a child, I spake as a child, I understood as a child, I thought as a child: but when I became a man, I put away childish things.

—1 CORINTHIANS 13:11

In verse 11, Paul draws the parallels between the maturing process of natural life and the growth process of the anointing. As we discussed earlier, the born-again experience is a refining process that doesn't end during this life. Ultimately, when that which is perfect comes on the day of the Lord, we will mature into our unfathomable glorified state, and the refining will then be complete. There was a time in my childhood that I didn't understand baptism, but I grew up.

Likewise, until recently, I didn't even believe in the continuation of the gifts, let alone know how to access them. But over time, I grew up and "put away" immature spiritual perspectives. Thanks to the anointing, I'm still growing today.

When we become spiritually mature men and women of God, we

put away the ignorance of our past and continue growing up, every day of our lives.

Second Peter 3:18 instructs us to "grow in grace, and in the knowledge of our Lord and Saviour Jesus Christ." You should know more about the Bible today than you did last month and access your anointing more this year than you did last year.

Hosea 4:6 says, "My people are destroyed for lack of knowledge." Notice that it doesn't say, "My people are destroyed for lack of opportunity," "My people are destroyed for lack of a good president," or "My people are destroyed for lack of resources."

The church has been spiraling into decay because we have become ignorant of the transforming power of the Word of God, especially regarding spiritual gifts. As a body, we stopped growing in understanding, stopped growing in faith, and stopped growing in power through the Holy Spirit's indwelling. We have to change all of that before it's too late.

The Role of Mystery

For now we see through a glass, darkly; but then face to face: now I know in part; but then shall I know even as also I am known.

—1 CORINTHIANS 13:12

In verse 12, while again pointing to the heavenly promises of the day of the Lord, Paul uses visual metaphors to reinforce the "glory to glory" nature of the anointing (2 Cor. 3:18). He's saying that the prophetic Word of God will remain somewhat cloudy to us till the very end, even as we grow in our knowledge and our understanding.

He's telling us that we're seeing things in a riddle, an enigma if you will. We're living through a divine mystery that can only be illuminated by the Holy Spirit, and even then, only in part. Likewise, this mystery can only be fully solved by Jesus, and that won't happen until He calls us into heaven.

When you look into a mirror, you can see yourself, but in reality, you only see a fraction of who you are. In this metaphor, your flesh produces a fogginess that makes it difficult to see rightly. This underscores our need to mature in Christ. We can talk about heaven, but since none of us has ever been there, we can't fully understand the experience.

We can visualize the glory of the throne of God and how every tribe, nation, and tongue will one day cast their crowns at the feet of the Lamb (Rev. 5:9), and we can sing about it, pray about it, preach about it, and prophesy about it, but we can only understand it in part. If you let that frustrate or discourage you, you'll miss the beauty of the process. Jesus is worthy of our pursuit, no matter how foggy our vision. It is to the glory of God that He wraps things in mystery, and it is an honor that He calls us to search them out (Prov. 25:2), even in part.

The Three Pillars of Christianity

> And now abideth faith, hope, charity, these three; but the greatest of these is charity.
>
> —1 CORINTHIANS 13:13

It is beautiful that God chose to end the love chapter this way. Faith, hope, and charity (love) are the three pillars of Christianity, and the greatest is love. He ends the chapter as He started it: If you sincerely want to access your anointing, you must first learn to love people as God loves people. Before you ask for signs and wonders or prophecies and wisdom—before you earnestly seek the highest gifts—you must answer this inescapable question. Do you really love people?

This entire chapter is about one foundational truth: We have nothing without love. The Holy Spirit stirred in the apostle Paul when the church was still an impossible dream, leading him to write the words that have come to embody Christianity through all generations. In all we do, we must walk in faith, hope, and—above all—love.

We all know that faith is a crucial fundamental, for without faith, it is impossible to please God (Heb. 11:6). After all, it's faith that gets us into heaven. Nonetheless, it's hollow without love. Likewise, hope is an anchor in the Bible and one of the greatest forces we will ever learn to grasp (Heb. 6:19), but through these words, God ensures we never make the mistake of placing it ahead of our active love for others. Nothing we can imagine, gain, grow, or share can rival the power of love.

No matter what comprises your mix of spiritual gifts—no matter how much mountain-moving faith you possess or undying hope you can take hold of—without love, you are just a clanging gong. Love is quite simply the key that unlocks the power of the Holy Ghost in your life.

Never forget this axiom: Nobody cares how much you know until they know how much you care. This truth has given greater liberty, power, and strength to me and my ministry than I ever dreamed possible, and I believe we're just now scratching the surface of all God has planned for us in these last days.

Why Is Love the Greatest of These?

Throughout the Bible, especially the New Testament, we see that love is the most important principled doctrine, but it's still reasonable to wonder why that's the case. Yes, from our perspective, "God is love" (1 John 4:16), but He could also be characterized as hope, faith, or even power.

After searching for the answer to this question, I've come to this overwhelming realization. Love is the very force that God uses to rescue all of us from our sin because it's the very same force that caused us to sin against Him to begin with. Let me explain.

Most people believe that the fall of man came through Adam's rebellion, but in reality, the cause was his love for Eve. In Genesis chapter 3, we learn that Eve was dramatically changed when she partook of the forbidden fruit, which compelled Adam to partake of the fruit as well. The Bible tells us that Eve was given unto her husband, Adam, and we learn that her body was dramatically transformed. Childbirth was suddenly possible for Eve, and she was also destined to die.

God had told Adam that if they ever ate of the forbidden fruit, they would "surely die" (Gen. 2:17), and Eve had just crossed that line. So, Adam had a choice. He could choose to live with God forever and let Eve die alone, or he could rebel against God to live and die with her. Adam was so overwhelmingly in love with his wife that, in the terror of the moment, he chose Eve over God. By doing so, Adam damned all his offspring—the entire human race across all generations—for love.

The First and the Last

Nearly every church you've ever visited preaches that Adam blamed Eve for the fall, but they're all wrong. When God asked Adam why he ate the fruit, he said Eve gave it to him (Gen. 3:12). But he wasn't answering in derogatory terms toward his wife. On the contrary.

When I study this story in spirit and truth, I hear Adam answering, in effect, "You know why I did it, Lord, for You gave me this woman to love and protect. So when I saw her change into this mortal form, I couldn't let her suffer a life in the wilderness apart from me. I love her, Lord, my God, and I couldn't let her die alone."

I well up with tears at the thought. Adam broke his connection with God to remain in connection with his wife, which is the gospel's prophetic origin. It's important to know that the apostle Paul also calls Jesus the second Adam or the "last Adam" (1 Cor. 15:45) to reveal this beautiful message. The reason that Jesus, the last Adam, had to redeem us through love is because the first Adam damned us through love.

This divinely written story about Jesus and His bride—the church—is about love. God redeems us from human love by the power of His agape love, and this is the love that must accompany the gifts if they are to find their purpose in *you*; for your family, the church, and this lost and dying world.

> Husbands, love your wives, even as Christ also loved the church, and gave himself for it; That he might sanctify and cleanse it with the washing of water by the word.
> —EPHESIANS 5:25–26

8

Supernatural Motivation

*I beseech you therefore, brethren, by the mercies of God,
that ye present your bodies a living sacrifice, holy, acceptable unto God, which is your reasonable service. And be
not conformed to this world: but be ye transformed by
the renewing of your mind, that ye may prove what is
that good, and acceptable, and perfect, will of God.*
—ROMANS 12:1–2

A S THE TITLE states, this short book is intended to serve as a
guide to *Accessing Your Anointing*. To ensure you learn more
about each type of gift, I encourage you to conduct your own
deeper personal study through the Bible passages cited throughout
the book. Do that, and you're sure to start operating according to
God's design for your life. For that reason, I won't be conducting a
full analysis of each of the three categories of gifting (manifestation,
ministry, and motivation) herein, but I'll surely revisit this ever-
expanding subject in a future text.

Having said that, I find it crucial that we all understand the gifts as they pertain to the motivational category. God gave motivational gifts for every single member of the body of Christ, so there's great value in understanding the strengths and weaknesses of each early in your journey. In Romans chapter 12, the apostle Paul delivers revelatory insights into this fascinating perspective.

Paul begins this key chapter by exhorting us by the mercies of God to commit to a life of service, holy and acceptable unto God, while avoiding any form of worldly behavior—either through our thoughts or actions. Keep that in mind as you grow in your gifting. Any amount of worldly behavior can short-circuit your anointing, so if you haven't yet crucified your flesh, please read *Weapons of Our Warfare* for effective strategies to that end.

A Law Worth Repeating

> For I say, through the grace given unto me, to every man that is among you, not to think of himself more highly than he ought to think; but to think soberly, according as God hath dealt to every man the measure of faith.
>
> —ROMANS 12:3

In verse 3 of our key chapter, Paul reminds us that—no matter who we are or how gifted we may be—none of this is about us. In John 15:5, Jesus said that we can do nothing without Him. This isn't our power that moves us; it's His. Likewise, in Galatians 6:3 we read, "For if a man think himself to be something, when he is nothing, he deceiveth himself."

It bears repeating that our gifts are for service to one another, not for selfish gain. If you use your gift selfishly, you'll regret it when you see God face to face. When we stand at the judgment seat of Christ on the day of the Lord, those who acted selfishly will answer for it, receiving wood, hay, and stubble, not the gold, silver, and precious stone that represent good treasures stored up for those who properly served Him (1 Cor. 3:11–15).

Likewise, if you don't use your gift, God will use someone with the same gift in your place who will steward it better (Matt. 25:14–30). You can't lose your gifting, but you can lose that element of your calling along with the resources God delivers to help you accomplish it.

Think and Grow According to Your Faith

In verse 3 of our key passage, Paul tells us not to think of ourselves more highly than we ought to but instead to "think soberly, according as God hath dealt to every man the measure of faith." He's not saying that it takes faith for some but not for others. He's saying that everyone is on a different level in their spiritual growth process. We mustn't compare ourselves to each other because, according to the Bible, "[they that compare] themselves among themselves, are not wise" (2 Cor. 10:12).

Some people have been born again for a long time, and others were born again just yesterday. Sadly, I know people who were just recently saved but are more Holy Spirit filled than people who claim to have been saved many years ago. Not everyone will get where you are overnight. For true growth to occur in the body of Christ, we cannot love people where we wish they were. We must love them where they're at.

I didn't get to where I am in twenty minutes, and some of the greatest saints I know took twenty years to truly catch fire. So we have to understand that growth is not a one-size-fits-all process. As one old-timer put it, "The same amount of food that will starve an elephant will stuff a mouse." Not everyone has the same capacity to handle what God has for them, but they will grow into that capacity by the measure of their faith.

> For as we have many members in one body, and all members
> have not the same office: So we, being many, are one body
> in Christ, and every one members one of another. Having
> then gifts differing according to the grace that is given to us,
> whether prophecy, let us prophesy according to the propor-
> tion of faith.
>
> —ROMANS 12:4–6

In verses 4 through 6 of our key passage, Paul tells us that the
purpose of the "one body" with many members is not human unity
but oneness in Christ. For that reason, I should never be jealous of
your gift. God gave it to you, and God gave *you* the grace to operate
in it. If I'm not given a particular gift, it's right to seek it and pray
for it, but entirely wrong to envy you or begrudge you for having it.

The ground is level at the foot of the cross, so we must rejoice in
each other's gifts, regardless of whether one seems greater or lesser.
Your gift is just as significant as mine, and all gifts are from God,
so we must be grateful for each, no matter who has them.

Another Brief Word on the Five-Fold Ministry

As you might recall, I generally discuss the spiritual gifts in three
categories: manifestation, ministry, and motivation. Up to now,
we've been studying them in the context of their manifestation, as
detailed in 1 Corinthians. As briefly noted earlier, the second category, ministry (also known as the five-fold ministry), offers perspective into church government and leadership, which reflects the
word "office" noted in Romans 12:4. We won't be diving into the
five-fold in this book, but let's read how Paul described them. He
said they are:

> For the perfecting of the saints, for the work of the ministry,
> for the edifying of the body of Christ: Till we all come in the
> unity of the faith, and of the knowledge of the Son of God,

unto a perfect man, unto the measure of the stature of the ful-
ness of Christ.

—EPHESIANS 4:12–13

Remember that these three categories of gifts overlap, so they
should never be viewed as boxes with a unique set of gifts in each,
but rather three different perspectives to help you understand them
and operate through them. As we turn toward the conclusion of
this book, we'll dive into the various ways the Holy Spirit anointing
motivates us to access His supernatural power.

The Gifts of Motivation

Having then gifts differing according to the grace that is
given to us, whether prophecy, let us prophesy according to
the proportion of faith; Or ministry, let us wait on our ministering: or he that teacheth, on teaching; Or he that exhorteth,
on exhortation: he that giveth, let him do it with simplicity;
he that ruleth, with diligence; he that sheweth mercy, with
cheerfulness.

—ROMANS 12:6–8

Unlike the gifts of manifestation, which the Holy Spirit activates
once we are born again, every man and woman alive is naturally
born with gifts of motivation (a.k.a. motivational gifts). As seen in
verses 6 through 8 of our key passage from Romans, there are seven
motivational gifts in total (seven being the number of completion
and maturity in the Bible), and each gift has unique strengths and
weaknesses.

A person may have a good mix of three or four of these seven
gifts, but each of us has one that stands out as our high-end gift
and another at the very low end of our spectrum that we struggle
to access even on our best days. Your high-end gift is a motivating
force that has affected and guided you from a very early age. As
you go through your process of growing your gifts, knowing and

understanding your strengths and weaknesses will help you to operate in proper alignment with them. Let's unpack the gifts of motivation as outlined in Romans 12:6–8.

Prophecy

Paul starts his list of motivational gifts with prophecy, the only gift mentioned in the three primary gifts chapters of the Bible: Ephesians 4, 1 Corinthians 12, and Romans 12. As you likely realize by now, folks in cessationist denominations believe this gift was only available to the prophets of the Old Testament. Having come out of that error, I get it, but the Holy Spirit and the Word of God have proven otherwise.

Paul instructs us on the gift of prophecy in the context of the New Testament church, not the Old Testament church—in three different books of the Bible—so ignoring these teachings today would be an act of disobedient ignorance to the Word. Never forget that Paul was merely a pen in God's hand, not the actual writer. These aren't Paul's suggestions to a handful of first-century Christians but God's commands for every believer until the day of judgment comes.

The strength of the gift of prophecy is that it gives its recipient an uncanny ability to discern the truth about seasons and people. Folks with this gift can speak a precise word about others without knowing Jack Spratt about them. They can discern your season and your past, and—once they're born again and operating through the anointing—they can discern whatever the Holy Spirit is doing or trying to do in your life. If you don't believe some people can be gifted this way, I'm sorry, but you have not been paying attention. I'll share a story at the conclusion of this book to help you see what I mean.

When discussing prophecy, as noted in an earlier chapter, I'm not talking about people who say they have the gift of discernment but are actually operating in a spirit of suspicion.

There's a massive difference between discernment and suspicion, as they're as far apart as right and wrong. Remember, love "beareth all things, believeth all things, hopeth all things" (1 Cor. 13:7), so there's no place for suspicion in the body of Christ.

The primary weakness that can be exposed in a person with a gift of prophecy is that they can easily appear or even become abrasive. If they're not careful, they can quickly develop a "holier than thou" mindset and perception without even realizing it, and they can slip into operating in their gift with the wrong motivation or the wrong spirit. When that happens, they typically hurt more people than they help. For this, Paul says, "Let us prophesy according to the proportion of faith" (Rom. 12:6).

Paul is saying that people who are strong in their faith can step into it with greater confidence that they're operating in the right spirit, while those new to the faith should focus more on growing their faith rather than operating in their gifting. First things first. Likewise, those who aren't even born again should simply allow their recognition of this gift to drive them to their knees to accept the gospel in repentance and get trained up in the ways of the Lord to keep things in proper order. No one should ever rush into operating in their gifting but wait for the Holy Spirit to guide them in accordance with the Scripture.

Don't Shy Away From the Process

It doesn't matter how weird, strange, and spooky this gift may seem to you. The supernatural power of God is supposed to blow our minds, so don't let your hesitation confuse you. Sometimes God simply reveals things to people with the gift of prophecy for the sake of His work in others.

When I was first waking up to the reality of the anointing, I was preaching at an anniversary celebration at Finish Line Christian Church in Mount Holly, North Carolina. During my sermon, I felt like the Lord was prompting me to release a specific word for someone. But I thought to myself, in doubt, "There are three hundred people in this room, and there is no way I can be sure who this is for," so I chickened out. I went on and preached a powerful message in accordance with the Holy Spirit but continued to doubt what I heard because it was so specific.

Lo and behold, after the service, the Lord corrected me while I was signing books and praying with people. A woman walked up to me for prayer and quickly revealed that she was in the exact situation I was supposed to call out during the service.

Consider how much more powerful that word would have been if I had delivered it to her from the altar of God.

Imagine if she had heard that word, realizing it was for her, and then stepped forward before all those witnesses rather than hearing me apologize for not having done so at the book signing table. Imagine how many more people in that church might have needed to see that move of God and hear that same message from God spoken over their lives.

Unfortunately, I was too timid to release the word that night, and in turn, I cheated a lot of people. In my insecurity, I somehow made it about me, but now I know better. I was learning to walk in this gifting, so the Lord used that moment to teach me something crucial about the anointing. If you're going to start to operate in your gifts with full obedience to the Scripture, sometimes you have to be willing to look stupid and do something that takes you way out of your comfort zone.

Reflecting on my ministry life, I can see many times when God gave me a word for someone, but I pulled back in timidity when I should have boldly pressed in. In hindsight, I wish I had been obedient and allowed my faith to increase by flowing in the anointing, as I've come to understand that overcoming these early hurdles of insecurity is part of the process.

The Gift of Ministry

Returning to our key passage, verse 7 is actually a lot simpler than it may read in King James English. When Paul wrote, "Or ministry, let us wait on our ministering," he's not saying let's just sit around and twiddle our thumbs and never get around to utilizing these gifts. In this context, the phrase *wait on* means to study, to learn, and to get trained up. He's saying while the Holy Spirit is still downloading the fullness of the gift—while God is still teaching you how to properly minister—you need to take your training very seriously.

Many people will sit around saying, "Well, one day, I'll get around to working on my gifting." No, I suggest that you get around to it right now. Too many folks are waiting to figure out the will of God for their lives when God is actually waiting for them to simply find a need and start to fill it. When in doubt, consider that as the default will of God. If you're in the right spirit, He'll guide you through it.

The gift of ministry is also known as the gift of helps. The strength of this gift is humility and selflessness. The folks with the gift of ministry don't feel the need to tell you how long it took them to do things as they serve because they simply enjoy serving God and others. If you want to pat them on the back, great, but they will *rock on* regardless of whether you praise them. Likewise, even if you criticize them, they'll usually just keep serving because they love to help and only aim to please God, not man.

The downside of folks with the gift of ministry or helps is that they tend to neglect their own need to receive ministry from others. They're like an ATM, always putting out but never receiving any deposits. Eventually, they go bankrupt. Remember the woman in

Mark chapter 5 who touched the hem of Jesus' garment? The Bible says that Jesus immediately felt virtue (power) come out of His body. When people touch you, they always drain something from you. The Bible says, "The devil leaveth him, and, behold, angels came and ministered unto him" (Matt. 4:11). Matthew was speaking of Jesus.

If Jesus needed ministry, how much more do we? The weakness in an overabundance of the gift of ministry is that folks tend to give and give and give, but they seldom take time to get refilled, and that's dangerous. There is something we call "spiritual equilibrium," which points to the need to avoid burning out. If we don't keep our spiritual balance, we'll eventually fall hard, and that hurts everyone, not just the person who falls. Folks with this gifting must learn to take in as much as they put out. If you want to have the fire burn brighter than ever before—if you want to increase your capacity to operate in this gift—you must learn to be fed properly by God.

The Gift of Teaching

Folks with the gift of teaching can take deep truths and boil them down in simplicity. Their students typically gain a fresher, deeper understanding of the Bible and, thereby, can easily apply these truths to their everyday lives. The biggest fallacy or abuse of the gift of teaching is intellectualism. I know people who are book-smart and God-dumb. They get so obsessed with their gift that they become useless to God, and unable to help anyone. They start to teach people things they're never even going to apply to their lives. As a teacher, I must ensure people truly understand and can apply what I'm teaching from the Bible. I never want folks walking away saying, "Wow, that was a powerful message, but I have no idea what he said."

Professing themselves to be wise, they became fools.
—ROMANS 1:22

Some of you have had a teaching gift all your life, even before you got saved. You could teach people how to change oil, change a tire, or do something on a computer. You could take high-level stuff that wasn't even spiritual and boil it down so people could understand it.

If you have the gift to become a teacher of the Bible, you must put even greater focus on this sort of practical application in people's lives. No one is impressed with your knowledge if people can't make it their own—least of all, God. Paul warned us to avoid teachers who profess themselves to be wise but in their lack of teaching skill, prove themselves to be fools (Rom. 1:22). Don't be like them.

The Gift of Exhortation

In verse 8 of our key passage, we find the gift of exhortation, also known as the gift of encouragement. Those of you born with this gift have been encouraging people all your life.

Before you even came to Christ, you simply loved to encourage people. Of course, we all should be encouragers, so no one is off the hook in this department, but some people have a far greater capacity to operate in this gifting all the time.

Those who exhort and encourage have a mindset always set on lifting others up. We have an elder in our congregation named Buford Bledsoe, and he is a prime example. When you get around him, or he prays over you, you simply can't walk away beat down. Folks with this gift consider others better than themselves (Phil. 2:3), so they are always helping others grow, even beyond their own capacity.

However, as is true of all motivational gifts, there's a weakness for those with the gift of exhortation. When they spend too much time alone, they can become very discouraged. Like those with the gift of helps (ministry), they tend to forget about their own need to be lifted up and ministered to by others, often failing to seek out the people they need to come alongside them to keep them encouraged.

I've seen this happen to folks many times, and there is something especially troubling about a discouraged encourager. How's that for a spiritual oxymoron? Like all the gifts, encouragers must work to learn to strike this delicate balance. When they do, they're especially beautiful and much-needed people in the body.

The Gift of Giving

Now we come into the realm of my highest gifting. Verse 8 of our key verse in Romans ends with, "he that giveth, let him do it with simplicity." To do it with simplicity means that it should be easy and simple to give generously to others. The people who operate in this gift have an understanding that it all belongs to God anyway, so they can give and give and never break a sweat.

I've talked a lot about stretching my faith in every way possible, but at the end of the day, giving is just simple and easy for me—but it's not so simple for everybody. God indeed loves a cheerful giver, but He'll still bless your giving even if you're a grouch about it (2 Cor. 9:6–7).

We all have a command and a mandate in the Bible to give, but for those who have this gift, it's simply who we are, so we can't help it. We were born this way. I was giving stuff away long before everyone was getting born again. But once I got born again, I just went crazy with my generosity. I started looking for ways to give stuff away even before I led a church blessed with high-level generosity. Giving is a core element of God's nature in Scripture. As Jesus taught us, "For God so loved the world that he gave his only begotten Son" (John 3:16). He didn't beg, borrow, steal, take, or loan—no, He *gave*. So if you truly love people, you give!

> Give, and it shall be given unto you; good measure, pressed
> down, and shaken together, and running over, shall men give
> into your bosom. For with the same measure that ye mete
> withal it shall be measured to you again.
>
> —LUKE 6:38

The downside for someone with the gift of giving, like me, is the difficulty we have with receiving. I like to give so much away that I can sometimes rob people of their blessing when I refuse to receive what they're trying to give me. For that, I often have to be reminded of what the Bible says in Luke 6:38: "Give, and it shall be given unto you." So, if you're going to learn to grow your gift as a giver, you must learn to be a good receiver. That's not easy for a giver.

It's a principle that all people need to learn, as it's all about good stewardship and the law of sowing and reaping (Gal. 6:7). You always reap what you sow, you always reap more than you sow, and you never reap a thing until you sow. This is true for everyone, but for some of us, the sowing is far easier than the reaping. If we hope to grow, we must also strike a balance with this gift.

Time-Out: A Holy Chain Reaction

By now, if you've never truly identified it, you're surely wondering about your own high-level gift and exactly what it is. Those who have been around a gift-recognizing church for any length of time will tell you that others in the church often recognized their top gift before they did. Certain folks in your local church will readily tell you about your gifting even when you don't ask for their opinion. You'll hear, "You sure have a discerning spirit," or "You sure are a good teacher."

God will use these folks to start dropping nuggets of confirmation in your life. And you'll soon realize that once you start properly operating in your gift, it will motivate those around you to do the same. That's why we call them motivational gifts. They motivate other people to up their access and use of all the gifts, even when it's not high on their gift spectrum.

I can prove that to you. Do you know why Global Vision Bible Church is one of the most generous churches on the planet? Because my high-end gift is operating at a high level, it's motivating the entire congregation to grow in that area. I'm the pastor, so that stands to reason. Every healthy church operating through the anointing will take on the personality and practice of gifts expressed at a high level by those who serve in the leadership and lay ministry.

The proper flow of the gifts simply sparks the gifts in every member. Isn't that beautiful? That's why the body is so important, and that's why your gift is for me, and my gift is for you. When you use your gift properly, you bless everyone in the church, far more than just the people you come in contact with.

The Gift of Administration

Continuing with verse 8 of our key passage, we see, "he that ruleth, with diligence." Did you know that ruling is a gift? The word *ruling* in this context (as used in the KJV) refers to what we commonly call the gift of administration. When people with this gift were just a year and a half old, they were probably already crawling around organizing toys or diapers in the nursery.

These people enjoy order and bless us all when they operate in it with proper balance. My high-end gift is giving, my secondary high-end gift would be teaching, and my third high-end gift would probably be mercy. The administration gift is not even on my spectrum. It's like the twelfth gift on my list, and there are only seven gifts, if you know what I mean.

The Gift of Mercy

My wife, Tai, is a tremendous teacher, but that's not her high-end gift. She's also a marvelous encourager, but that isn't her high-end gift either. Her high-end gift is easily the gift of mercy, as she can be merciful and kind to people that I don't even want to be kind to. This gift offers an especially poignant example of the danger we can face when we don't maintain proper balance in its operation. For example, the slippery slope, or the downside of mercy, is that they can easily compromise what's best for everyone just to exhibit their mercy, and doing so is to the detriment of all involved.

I know I give Joel Osteen a hard time, but I'm not really against what Joel says. I'm against what he doesn't say. He's an encourager, and his high-end gift is mercy, but when someone has a combination of mercy and encouragement at the high end of their spectrum, they tend to compromise in areas crucial to the church's health.

When you lean too hard in that direction, you usually struggle to take a bold stand on biblical truth when it's needed most, simply because it's uncomfortable for the congregation—and even more uncomfortable for the person with the high-end gift of mercy. For a pastor with a lot of influence and a large audience, that can be disastrous.

Folks with this gift at the high end of their spectrum must be careful not to be over-merciful, or they'll end up compromising and contradicting the Bible's clear teachings. This is why your gift and my gift are to sharpen each other, for as we learn in the Proverbs, "Iron sharpeneth iron; so a man sharpeneth the countenance of his friend" (Prov. 27:17).

The Use of the Gifts in Unity

For where two or three are gathered together in my name,
there am I in the midst of them.

—MATTHEW 18:20

Gathering and properly operating through our gifts, in Jesus' name, defines oneness (godly unity) in a local church body. Our collective use of our gifts invites the presence of God from heaven into our midst, and that's the true essence of oneness.

When you properly operate in your gifts, you reveal who you are in Christ, and your thought processes and decisions begin to align with His with beautiful impact in every aspect of your life.

Likewise, the Holy Spirit begins to guide the way you choose your friends and all those who influence your life. The refining fire begins to burn on full tilt, and the pruning process brings forth great fruit. All of this is sparked through the power of God-given motivation, and each of us must embrace it in the context of the body of Christ if we hope to bless the Lord and all those we are called to love.

I find it interesting and troubling that folks can live their entire lives knowing that they reap what they sow (Gal. 6:7) and even go to church every Sunday and Wednesday but never operate in the gifts they were born with. We each have at least one motivational gift that God needs us to access to fulfill our personal calling, and every one of these gifts is eternally valuable, just as every one of us is eternally valuable to Him.

When you operate in your gift, it allows me to fully operate in mine, and this is a transaction that moves God's heart on behalf of all. When we all access our anointing in fullness, together as one, the result is the perfecting of the saints, the work of the ministry, and the edifying of the body of Christ (Eph. 4:12). I need you, you need me, and we all need Him. This is the glory-infused unity that comes from His indwelling—the anointing—that Jesus prayed into every believer through His final discourse before the cross.

> Neither pray I for these alone, but for them also which shall believe on me through their word; That they all may be one; as thou, Father, art in me, and I in thee, that they also may be one in us: that the world may believe that thou hast sent me. And the glory which thou gavest me I have given them; that they may be one, even as we are one: I in them, and thou in me, that they may be made perfect in one; and that the world may know that thou hast sent me, and hast loved them, as thou hast loved me.
>
> —JESUS (JOHN 17:20–23)

CONCLUSION

M Y DEAR FRIEND Brian Gibson, who wrote the foreword to this book, pastors a church with several locations around the country. He recently invited me to a gathering at their campus in Kentucky where a guy from the nation of Colombia would be ministering.

Brian told me that the minister was known as Prophet Gustavo and that he didn't know English but spoke through an interpreter.

I've been open about my difficult journey into the spiritual gifts, and I will remain that way as I bring this book to a close.

In the not-so-distant past, I would have thought Gustavo's ministry was absolutely crazy. I would have called it out as smoke and mirrors spooky-kooky nonsense, but this is a new season in my life, and I trust Brian completely. He convinced me to show up and enjoy the service and said, "This guy might not even say one word to you. He's just planning to preach, but maybe God has something for you." I was curious, but I also remember thinking, "What have I gotten myself into?"

I'm so busy traveling in our ministry that I don't typically attend someone else's service unless scheduled to teach. I speak somewhere around the country pretty much every day of the week, and I never miss Sundays or Wednesdays at Global Vision, so I simply don't have time to sit and receive. But this time, I felt compelled to do just that.

We arrived early because Tai is an amazing worshiper who never lets us miss the music. Halfway into a song, I saw this normal-looking guy walk in and sit down among all the people. I assumed it was him, but I wasn't sure. Soon thereafter, Brian introduced him as Gustavo, and the guy just started talking about the fact that a spoken word and the written Word of God would never contradict each other, so he was already speaking my language. He then went on to say that we've been taught that a prophetic word is a "thing," even though it's a person—Jesus Christ. That got my attention.

It was a beautiful message, and it was as doctrinally sound as it could be. He cited John 1 and said, "The Word became flesh and dwelt among us." This was a message I would have preached even in my cessationist days. So far, so good. About halfway through the message, he started to walk over to people and read their mail. It was eye-opening.

Again, I am going to be honest. There was a time I would have been like, "This is wacky," and I would have wanted to look away. Through his interpreter Ricardo, Gustavo said, "I'm here to tell you that what's wrong with a lot of you is that you believe a lot of witchcraft and sorcery in the church. This witchcraft caused you to ignore what the Word of God says, so now, when God gives someone a word of wisdom or a word of knowledge for you, it freaks you out."

At this point, I'm thinking, "Wow, he is spot on." That's exactly why I didn't believe and search it out in the past, dismissing it as spooktacular foolishness. But he had nearly everyone he spoke to in a puddle of tears and didn't know any of them from Adam, so I couldn't look away. I mean, I was riveted. It was clear that these people needed to hear every word of it.

I preach everywhere, and I've seen every trick there is. I understand car salesman manipulation and the darkness in the power of suggestion. I know we must be careful, so my antennas were way up at this time. Gustavo continued preaching in a big way, and he would stop and go right back into the Word of God and then right back to preaching while his interpreter flowed with him the entire time. It was powerful.

I sat there with Tai, silently saying to God, "I hope this is the real deal. Lord, I don't know how long this cat is gonna go, but if what he's saying is real, and if You have a word for me, then I need him to come over, lay hands on me, and give me that word. If this is real, make him call me out on something in front of all these people."

Not five minutes after praying that to the Lord, it happened. Gustavo walked over to me, stood right in front of me, laid his hand on my head, and said through the interpreter, "Through you flows a gift of the prophetic." Then suddenly he did something totally unexpected that proved to me that he was legit. Before he could finish his sentence, he abruptly stopped, shook his head as if to say no, and then turned to Tai. With his hand on her head, he said, "Through YOU, there is a gift of the prophetic, and through him (pointing back to me) flows the Word" (referring to the gifts of wisdom and knowledge).

I'm telling you, it was the most surreal moment of my ministry life up to that time. I've had people say that I'm a prophet, and I understand the prophetic—especially after preparing for and writing this book—but I've never really walked in it or flowed in it. But my wife is a different story. She's the one who flows in the prophetic, albeit in private, and there's no way this guy knew that because she hasn't yet stepped into it in public.

Then Gustavo said to her, "You have been good for him, and he has been good for you because you flow in the prophetic, and he flows in the Word. And since the Word of God is supposed to be prophetic, when these two shall become one flesh, you have a spirit of prophecy in your home and can preach prophetically. You're able to be bold and say things that many people can't say."

It didn't stop there. He walked over to Brian and started speaking over him, and then came back to me, grabbed me by the hand, and pulled me up in front of everybody. My palms got sweaty. Then he said, "You have been a man of books. You've read books and read books and read books, and you've put God in a box all those years."

By now, you know this part of my testimony. I was so Baptist born and Baptist bred that I figured when I died, I'd be Baptist dead. I believed being Baptist was the first-class seat on the plane to eternity. That's all I ever knew most of my life, and all of this would have seemed like utter charismatic nonsense just a while ago. But not now. Then he brought Tai up to join me, reiterated his word about her prophetic gifting meshing with my word gifting, and said, "Now God is going to take you out of the box, and God is going to elevate your church more than what you've already seen… more people are going to come, and you'll see more miracles, more signs, more wonders, more baptisms, more salvations, and more healings in a greater movement of the Spirit of God."

Maybe you're thinking, "Well, Pastor Locke, I see why that would inspire you, but maybe he was just encouraging you the way any good man or woman could. Maybe he's heard of you and knows about the revival breaking out at your church. Maybe there was nothing supernatural about it."

In all fairness, if this were the full story, I'd have to admit you have a point. But he still wasn't finished. What he said next sealed the deal between God and me. Inexplicably, Gustavo said, "When you were eight months old in your mother's womb, you weren't supposed to be born, and the devil tried to kill you because there was a call on your life. But when you grew into a young man, God called you to the ministry."

He was correct. In 1967, when my mama was eight months pregnant and very young, she went to an abortion clinic out of desperation, but against all reasonable logic, the abortion doctor himself talked her out of it. Praise God. Gustavo then told me that I was sixteen years old when I was called into the ministry. Right again. He kept on telling me things he had no rational way of knowing. This guy was visiting from South America and honestly didn't know anything about me. Let me add that this sort of confirmation shouldn't even be necessary when the Spirit is moving through someone with this gift, but the Lord knew what I needed to fully receive it, once and for all.

Then Gustavo did something especially beautiful. He gestured with his jacket and began talking about Elijah passing the mantle to Elisha, referring to the symbolic power of that moment in the Bible record. At this point, my hands were shaking, and Tai and I were both crying. Though I fully believed the Lord was speaking through him, I couldn't stop thinking about how unbelievable this was.

Then he started telling us about our home, and he began prophesying things about our daughter (that he had no reason to know even existed) and talked about the anointing upon her that would shake people. Our family already knows this, but there's no way he knew. He said, "There's a lot of noise in your life right now, there are a lot of people against you right now, and there's a lot of this happening in and around your church."

As we stood there in front of the congregation, he then put his jacket over both of our heads and said, "I feel like the Lord wants me to tell you, you are no longer going to see the attacks of the enemy, you are no longer going to pay attention to what the news media says, and you're no longer going to scroll through social media and waste any more energy or sleep. God is going to put men and women around you that are going to protect you, that are going to be so surrendered to the work of God and the ministry of the local church, that they're going to undergird you, hold you up, and strengthen you."

It was one of the most powerful, fire-filled, life-changing services I've ever experienced, and I was just one of many in attendance who experienced this sort of life change that night—simply for being willing to give God the right to move through one man's gifting. There's no way around the fact that everything he said was 100 percent correct, and the others in attendance concurred. As spooky as this sort of ministry was to me in the past, I learned that night that when the anointing flows through a willing vessel—speaking something the Holy Spirit wants to say to you—you won't be able to deny it.

As I meditated over all of this with the Lord, I asked Him if there could be a less abrasive way to fulfill my role in this great mission. Maybe the haters are right about me. Maybe I *am* crazy. Do I want to keep putting my family and church through all this warfare? Likewise, do I want to draw even greater hate from the religious crowd by stepping into the supernatural activity of the anointing?

As I sat there reflecting on all of this, I recalled John the Baptist's moment of raw transparency and doubt as he sat rotting in prison, awaiting his inevitable execution. While imprisoned, John began struggling with his stark reality, and he eventually sent messengers to ask Jesus if He was the Messiah after all. He had to be wondering if he was simply deluded to have believed it—crazy to have put his life on the line for a battle that might not have been his to begin with (Luke 7:18–35).

Try to visualize John at that time. The fiery-bold preacher of God, whom Jesus called the greatest prophet to ever be born of a woman, sitting there listless, looking through the bars of a cold, dank dungeon in the bowels of Herod's palace while the enemy wracked his mind and body in every way imaginable. It had to be a brutally desperate moment, yet those words surely fall short of the pain and fear that must have swept over him in his darkest hours.

In my moment of second-guessing, I related to John in new ways. It was sobering. Then I remembered how Jesus responded, and God used that moment of reflection to remind me of the crossroads we all have to pass when He calls us to finally step into our calling in full. As He did for John in his days of self-doubt, God sent His messenger Gustavo to say exactly what He said to the Baptist, and I could hear Him telling the prophet on that night, "Hey, man of God, I want you to give this word to Greg Locke…tell him that the blind see, the lame walk, the lepers are cleansed, the deaf hear, the dead are raised, and the gospel is preached to the poor!" And to that, I said to Him, once and for all, "Yes, Lord!"

You are the living God! I will doubt you no longer! I receive Your commission, I will walk in Your anointing, and I will never confuse Your Word again! Teach me and send me, Lord!

> But the Comforter, which is the Holy Ghost, whom the Father will send in my name, he shall teach you all things, and bring all things to your remembrance, whatsoever I have said unto you.
>
> —Jesus (John 14:26)

The Starting Point

This is just the beginning of what God is doing in His church. Like the content of this book, we're just now scratching the surface of where God wants to take us in the Bible. Our redemption is drawing nigh, and the day of the Lord is coming quickly upon us. This lost and dying world is crying out, and there is an untapped power in the body of Christ. It is time to wake up the sleeping church and step into His supernatural call.

The church is preparing to go through a refining process that will burn away the chaff and birth a power that has never been seen before, but we cannot forget that the process is difficult. It will require many of us to turn from everything we have ever known— in the blink of an eye. Jesus said, "Because strait is the gate, and narrow is the way, which leadeth unto life, and few there be that find it" (Matt. 7:14). To be chosen by God and stand among the few, to rise within the remnant church in these last of the last days, will require the same level of sacrifice, surrender, faith, hope, and love that marked Jesus and His chosen in the first century. Are you ready?

Please Pray This With Me

Father, thank You for Your Word. Thank You for its infal-libility and how it corrects us when we have been theo-logically and philosophically wrong. We know the Bible is a book of freedom, and we know in Galatians 5:1 You tell us, "Where the Spirit of the Lord is, there is liberty," so I pray Your liberty for all who are reading this book. May we marinate in the Word and be reminded that it doesn't matter what we're able to accomplish if it's not done in love. For without You, our efforts have no eternal value. Bless all we studied in this book, and may it make us all free. Father, we thank You for the understanding of our spiritual gifts and Your anointing that empowers them. May we discover them, sense them, grasp them, earnestly seek them, and operate through them according to Your holy design. You've loosed some people with this teaching, Lord, so we cry out as You did at the tomb of Lazarus, "Loose him and let him go!" And Lord, after we have come to the truth, may You unleash the anointing on a sleeping church to finally rise into her calling as Your bride, the beautiful, spotless bride for which You'll soon return, tried and true and filled with Your Holy Spirit fire and power. In Jesus' name, amen.

To be continued...